Making Sense
of Social Security Reform

Making Sense of Social Security Reform

Daniel Shaviro

The University of Chicago Press
Chicago & London

DANIEL SHAVIRO is professor of law at New York University and author of *Do Deficits Matter?* (1997) and *When Rules Change: An Economic and Political Analysis of Transition Relief and Retroactivity* (2000).

THE UNIVERSITY OF CHICAGO PRESS, CHICAGO 60637
THE UNIVERSITY OF CHICAGO PRESS, LTD., LONDON

09 08 07 06 05 04 03 02 01 00   1 2 3 4 5
ISBN: 0-226-75116-3 (cloth)

Library of Congress Cataloging-in-Publication Data

Shaviro, Daniel N.
    Making sense of Social Security reform / Daniel Shaviro.
      p. cm.
    Includes bibliographical references and index.
    ISBN 0-226-75116-3
      1. Social security—United States.   2. Social security—Finance—
Government policy—United States.   I. Title.

HD7125 .S526 2000
368.4'3' 00973—dc21   00-021709

For Pat, Peter, and Charles

Contents

Acknowledgments

....

I am grateful to Geoffrey Huck for suggesting and encouraging this project, and to Joseph Bankman, David Bradford, Stephen Cohen, Geoffrey Huck, Kenneth Simonson, and two anonymous reviewers for their comments on earlier drafts.

❚ Introduction

Plans to reform Social Security are as plentiful, and to much of the public about as welcome, as Christmas fruitcakes. Most people realize that a slowly building long-term fiscal imbalance, persisting despite recent budget surpluses, makes change to the Social Security system inevitable. While perhaps fearing that things are bound to get worse, few have good information about the real policy choices that our representatives in Washington will be making in the next few years and how these choices might affect us.

Even the current Social Security system is poorly understood by most people who are subject to it. Try finding someone who has a good grasp on how current work decisions will affect his or her future Social Security benefits. When the subject turns to Social Security reform, the level of public confusion if anything deepens. Those who have tried to follow the Washington policy debate may have heard of such competing proposals as "privatization," "investing the budget surplus in Social Security," and "investing the Social Security Trust Fund in the stock market." What these really mean and how we should even try to think about them are questions that few understand.

Public political discussion of Social Security reform has mainly taken place at the level of bland and close to meaningless abstraction. We hear about the importance of "saving Social Security," but what does "saving" it mean? And what exactly are we saving? Suppose you had $1,000 coming to you through Social Security on the day you retired, but the system lacked the money to pay for this benefit. Would it count as "saving Social Security" to make you pay $1,000 to the system the day before you retired so that the system could hand this money back to you the next day? Absurdly enough, this actually would meet the definition of "saving Social Security" that has dominated the public political debate about possible changes.

The battling flotillas of experts sailing into the fray have often done little to advance public understanding of the real issues raised by Social Security reform. To be fair, an outstanding economic literature on Social Security has emerged in recent years, and I draw on it extensively while also seeking to contribute to it. However, ideological axes to grind have led some good economists, apparently excited by the policy stakes, to practice bad economics when engaged in public political discussion of possible changes. In addition, some expert discussion, like that among politicians, is so confined to events that can be defined as occurring within the official boundaries of the "Social Security system" that its real-world relevance brings to mind the debate between two atheists, described in the novel *Catch-22*, concerning what, if there were a God, He would be like.

This book aims to provide a clear picture of the issues posed by Social Security reform. To be sure, I cannot claim to be ideologically an empty vessel. As the reader will see, I tend to combine sympathy for markets and letting people make their own choices (often typical of a conservative) with sympathy for progressive redistribution (often typical of a liberal). However, I will neither make a fetish of these leanings nor let them drive the analysis in concealed ways. Instead, my aim will be to describe the real policy choices that we face and the main arguments bearing on how to make these choices, noting my own preferences where appropriate but mainly steering clear of outright advocacy.

My basic strategy for clarifying the issues raised by Social Security reform is twofold. In order to understand and evaluate such abstractions as "the Social Security system" or "privatization," we must both break them down into their salient parts and conceptually integrate them with the surrounding fiscal and economic landscape. Thus, I engage in both decomposition—or separating the parts—and integration, or evaluating what Social Security really does in light of its interaction with other government programs and the economy.

Decomposition, or, Not Missing the Trees for the Forest

Social Security is a multipurpose system, and virtually all proposals to change it have multiple types of effects. A failure to separate these out can leave you with a falsely limited sense of our actual choices, at the limit suggesting that we must either keep it essentially the same (restoring solvency aside) or radically transform it, rather than deciding one by one which of its features we like. Even insofar as the polar choice between "saving" and "privatizing" Social Security is concerned, pundits on all sides tend to be swayed unduly by their emotional responses to the system's New Deal origins and symbolic status as an exemplar of government activism, to the point where genuine policy differences are lost behind passionate concerns about mere packaging.

This is an area where we often do not really have a clear sense of what we are talking about. The current Social Security system is enshrouded in myth by the grace of not only its history, but the sheer inscrutability of what exactly it is doing at any time, as between giving people back their own tax contributions and redistributing lifetime net wealth. This inscrutability, by making retirees' benefits seem at once earned and yet a bonanza, has long helped make Social Security the proverbial "third rail of American politics" for those who dare to propose tampering with it—a status that is denied to more transparent portions of our fiscal system, such as the income tax and pork barrel spending.

I will explain, however, that Social Security's core retirement program— throughout this book I set to one side its related disability program—is simply a wage tax during one's working years followed by a wage subsidy (since benefits depend on wages) upon retirement, leaving some people with a net wage tax and others with a net wage subsidy. The retirement program is best conceptualized as combining three main functions. The first is forced saving, insofar as your tax contributions (or those of others) are used to give you retirement benefits that you cannot spend sooner. The second is limiting portfolio choice regarding how to save, since participants cannot, for example, invest their forced saving in the stock market in the hope of increasing what they will get at the price of accepting greater risk. The third function is redistribution, insofar as some people get back more than the value of their tax contributions while others get back less.[1]

In many cases, people who complain about the meager return that Social Security is offering them on their tax contributions fail to understand—although of course they need not like or accept—how this reflects the redistributive element of current Social Security policy, rather than how their forced saving is being invested. In addition, they may be misled by focusing just on how Social Security treats them, as distinct from how they fare overall under our fiscal system. After all, they would not gain from increasing their Social Security returns but at the same time increasing by the same amount their liability under the income tax.

For another example of the importance of breaking ideas down into smaller parts, consider the adage that Social Security provides "social insurance" by guaranteeing the elderly, or at least those among them who have worked, a minimum level of retirement income. We will see that the notion of "social insurance" has multiple relevant dimensions, some of which the current system performs better than others. To some extent, "social insurance" involves not insurance in the strict economic sense of risk-spreading, but risk prevention through limits on individual choice. Consider automobile accident risks, which we address in part by saying that children and drunks cannot drive and through speed limits and seat belt rules. Similarly, Social Security, to the extent it forces to you save and prevents you from choosing speculative investment vehicles, impedes certain individual choices that, in a worst-case scenario, could leave you with no retirement income. The manner and extent of these limitations on individual choice are potentially subject to considerable fine-tuning, depending on how well you think people choose for themselves, but this requires a clearer focus on the choice issues than has been usual in public debate.

"Insurance" in a strict economic sense refers to spreading or pooling risk across a large population. Thus, a group of automobile drivers may pool their accident risks (typically with an insurance company acting as the intermediary) so that anyone who has an accident will not be financially obliterated. By contrast, if one driver agreed or was compelled to pay in full for another's accidents along with his own, this would not be true insurance in an aggregate social sense (although the benefited driver would presumably regard himself as insured). Risk would only have been shifted, not diffused.

As we will see, in some respects Social Security is a true risk-spreading system. For instance, like the income tax and such income-conditioned transfer programs as welfare benefits and Food Stamps, it mitigates income risk by redistributing some of the proceeds of relative good fortune. In other respects, however, it merely transfers risk from one group to another. Historically, its implicit deal has roughly been that benefits for those who are near or past retirement age can go up but not down as current fiscal conditions warrant. This arrangement, rather than spreading between the young and the old the risk of economic and demographic changes that alter the program's long-term solvency, gives the elderly a part of the upside but the young the entire downside.

One last example (for now) of decomposition concerns "privatization," which we will find is no unitary thing but rather a conglomeration of three conceptually distinct policy changes (with accompanying administrative and bookkeeping changes) that could be adopted or not in any combination. One policy change is increasing Social Security's advance funding in the hope that this will correlate with increasing national saving. The second is increasing portfolio choice within the Social Security system. The third is eliminating redistribution through Social Security, whether between generations or from high earners to low earners within a generation.

Different people may favor none, some, or all of these distinct changes to the current system. I will show, for example, how privatization could be modified to address only saving and consumer choice, while retaining or even increasing the current level of progressive redistribution. Public political debate, by treating privatization as a single take-it-or-leave-it package, has discouraged thinking in such flexible terms.

Integration, or, Not Mistaking the Forest for the Entire Landscape

Think again about the idea of "saving Social Security." This focus on the supposed needs of a system brings to mind the "pathetic fallacy" in literature, which "holds that nature is like us, that it is endowed with feelings, moods, and goals we can understand" (Delgado and Stefancic 1992, 1261). What nature was to the nineteenth century (the high point of the pathetic fallacy), Social Security seems to be to the early twenty-first. An accident victim will suffer if we do not save him, but a system?

Undoubtedly, those who want to save, or for that matter slay, Social Security really do understand that what matters is the people whom it affects, not the system itself. They often seem to forget, however, that overall effects on people are therefore what matters in Social Security reform. Indeed, the tendency to think myopically just about Social Security is so pervasive that a little story is in order, to dramatize the problem and provide a useful catchphrase.

Mr. and Mrs. Clown—the Clown family—are hardworking folk, but not the best financial planners. They run a corner grocery store in the form of a proprietorship from which they take all the profits and are liable to pay all the debts. They observe that the store has begun to lose money and that their savings are therefore dwindling.

"What should we do?" Mr. Clown asks.

Mrs. Clown replies: "It's no wonder we're losing money. What do you expect when you consider that we've been working for free? We need to start paying ourselves decent living salaries."

So they start paying themselves $2,000 a month each and consider themselves lucky to have gotten their own services so cheap. The salary is nice, but then they notice that the grocery store has begun losing $4,000 more per month than previously.

What to do now? Hard times demand belt-tightening all around. So they call themselves in for a meeting and agree to a temporary pay cut.

The Clowns also notice that their personal expenses have been high. Every Saturday night they have been eating in expensive restaurants, with Mr. Clown paying for the meals on his credit card. This problem calls for another little meeting.

"My credit card bills are too high," says Mr. Clown. "We need to cut back."

"You're absolutely right," says Mrs. Clown. "Should we stop going out to dinner so frequently, or at least go to cheaper restaurants?"

"Ouch!" Mr. Clown replies. "We really enjoy those dinners . . . I've got it! Why don't we carry on as before, except that every other week *you* charge the dinner bill on *your* credit card? That way, neither of our credit card bills will be as high as the one I had last month."

Ultimately, Mr. and Mrs. Clown go bankrupt and thus learn the hard way about the importance of looking at the whole picture. Yet none of their decisions in response to the family fiscal crisis actually hurt, apart from distracting their attention. Their decisions merely failed to help. Salary is a wash if you pay it to yourself, and excessive outlays are unaffected by spreading them differently among your credit cards. The Clowns got a false picture by looking only at the salaries they received or paid, or only at their highest individual credit card bill.

I will henceforth use the term "Clown family accounting" to describe this sort of myopia, whereby one mistakes a part of one's finances for the whole and thus erroneously views a shift between the parts as significant overall. To be sure, Clown family accounting has very different implications for the federal government than for the Clowns. It betokens not bankruptcy, since the government can always raise taxes or walk away from commitments that are not legally binding, but simply a failure to choose intelligently between priorities. For example, if we address an overall fiscal imbalance simply by changing what we attribute to the Social Security Trust Fund, we will still have to deal with the imbalance in the long run, only with less advance warning and fewer options. And if we choose a particular financing response, such as a Social Security tax increase or benefit cut, simply because we are fixated on the Trust Fund, we may miss the opportunity to ask more fundamentally how we want to share benefits and burdens among our citizens.

Clown family accounting is a major feature in most public political discussions of the Social Security Trust Fund and its adequacy to pay for projected future benefits. The only genuine feature of such discussions arises because, if there are enough Clown family accountants in Congress, what we attribute to the system as an arbitrary accounting matter may actually affect substantive political decisions. This widespread belief that accounting matters gives rise to what I call the "Cowardly Lion effect." Just as, in *The Wizard of Oz*, the Cowardly Lion may actually have become brave once the Wizard gave him a medal for extraordinary valor, so a mere bookkeeping transaction may affect future political decisions because people treat it as meaningful.

Cowardly Lion effects—a more sympathetic term might be "earmarking"—can indeed be real. However, we must be careful not to confuse them with things that matter directly. And we should also keep in mind some caveats about earmarking's significance. Its efficacy depends both on whether future political decision makers decide to respect it even nominally and on the extent to which it really constrains them. Suppose, for example, that they could use the Social Security Trust Fund to pay for a totally different set of programs by simply labeling those programs as part of "Social Security." Or suppose they used quadruple income taxation of Social Security benefits to renege indirectly on the commitments we thought we were foisting on them by boosting the Trust Fund. More generally, the plasticity of official labels and the multitude of fiscal instruments available to the government may reduce earmarking's efficacy even if we feel confident enough about our capacity to determine good future policy to be legitimately interested in employing it.

Some Principles to Remember

In analyzing the issues raised by Social Security reform, I will mostly steer clear of the details of particular proposals by various politicians and policy entrepreneurs. These no doubt will continue to proliferate as long as Social Security reform commands public attention. In addition, I will give only brief and general attention to the numbers—revenue estimates, proposed tax rates, years before official system insolvency, and the like—that typically are emphasized in Social Security discussions. These numbers often provide only a misleading sense of precision and are subject to continual change anyway. Finally, I will only briefly explore the "transition path" question of exactly how to get from the current system to a preferred future one. Travelers generally do not plan their routes until they have decided where they want to go.

Two closely related cardinal principles will guide my inquiry, and I will argue that they should guide everyone's. They may seem simple, and by the end of this book perhaps even crushingly obvious, yet so far in the Social Security debate they have often been ignored.

The first cardinal principle is: *Don't change the basic structure of the Social Security system just to restore its solvency—do it, if at all, to improve the policy.* One can in fact restore the fiscal sustainability of Social Security and other long-term government programs through a host of small-bore changes that involve no significant rethinking of our general policy aims. This would be a mistake, however, because Social Security and related programs contain a great deal of relatively hidden and misunderstood policy that possibly could be improved. A good example may be provided by the system's adverse treatment of two-earner couples relative to one-earner couples. It should take no fiscal crisis for us to want to improve what we are doing, and we should keep this aim in mind even if the funding crisis evaporates.

The second cardinal principle is: *Don't treat the achievement of projected system solvency as the aim of Social Security reform—the aim, rather, should be to have a good fiscal system.* If the problem were simply a need to increase the amount officially credited to the Social Security Trust Fund so it is large enough to pay for all currently promised benefits, we could do this at the stroke of a pen—say, by announcing that from now on each dollar paid into this system will count, for bookkeeping purposes, as three dollars. This approach is not far from what political leaders and even prominent economists have proposed, yet its only possible real-world significance is as a nonbinding policy statement concerning what future Congresses should do. Even to the extent that such a bookkeeping maneuver can genuinely raise the probability that Social Security benefits will in fact be paid, we ought to ask: What makes us so sure they should be? What choices and tradeoffs will we face in the future, and how else might the money be spent, whether in providing for Americans' retirement or more generally? Do we even help people by guaranteeing their Social Security benefits if they end up paying for the benefits in full through other tax increases or benefit cuts?

Road Map for the Rest of the Journey

The basic plan for the rest of this book is as follows: Chapter 2 discusses the basic tax and benefit rules that are Social Security's main building blocks. Chapter 3 shows that these rules are best thought of as resulting in forced saving and limited portfolio choice plus or minus a transfer. Chapter 4 discusses the fundamental issues of social insurance that Social Security implicates. Chapter 5 looks at the Social Security Trust Fund and issues of long-term system financing, including proposals that go by the Clown family–inflected name of "investing budget surpluses in the Trust Fund." Chapter 6 discusses "traditionalist" proposals to restore Social Security's long-term solvency without changing it fundamentally, including suggestions that Trust Fund proceeds be invested in the stock market. Chapter 7 discusses privatization. Each of these chapters includes a brief summary of its discussion at the end. And finally chapter 8 provides an overall conclusion and discusses the rough outlines of an alternative proposal of my own that I call progressive privatization.

2 The Basic Building Blocks: Social Security Taxes and Benefits

Social Security is one government program that directly affects everyone. It taxes the first dollar earned by a minimum wage worker and later in life may serve as a vital defense against poverty. If you have a reasonably successful and full-time work career followed by a long retirement, the total cash flow first from you to the system and then the other way will run into the hundreds of thousands of dollars. These are amounts that matter, unless perhaps you are as rich as Bill Gates or as spiritual as Mother Teresa.

Accordingly, both as a worker and as a voter, you may want to understand Social Security's basic design features. What rules determine the amounts that you first pay and then get? What personal characteristics or decisions would tend to make you a big Social Security winner or loser? And from a design standpoint, where does the system fit on the continuum from well-oiled machine to Rube Goldberg monstrosity?

The Social Security Portion of the Payroll Tax

Other than the federal income tax, the federal payroll tax is by far the largest levy in the United States. If you get a regular pay stub, a little arithmetic will show that your employer, in order to pay your share of this tax, has withheld from it 7.65 percent of your stated wages up to an annual ceiling, which for 1999 stood at $72,600. Although not shown on your pay stub, the employer also pays its own 7.65 percent payroll tax on your earnings up to the ceiling.[1] Above the ceiling, the payroll tax continues, but its rate is reduced to 1.45 percent on each side of the employment transaction.

Economists generally agree that the distinction in who pays which portion of the payroll tax has no effect on economic incidence, and that at least in the short run the entire tax is largely borne by workers (Rosen 1995, 285–86). Thus, in your thinking about the payroll tax, you should combine the employer's nominal share with your own and deem it a single 14.2 percent levy on your earnings up to the ceiling. This is the percentage determined by adding together the two nominal shares at 7.65 percent but adjusting for the exclusion of the employer share from the wage base on which it is levied.[2]

In official government accounts, the payroll tax finances not only Social Security but also Medicare. The Social Security portion is deemed to be just a 6.2 percent tax on both the worker and the employer up to the annual ceiling, and nothing above that. Thus, the "Social Security tax" has two rate brackets: 11.5 percent (combining the two nominal shares but adjusting for exclusion of the employer share from the base) up to the annual ceiling, and zero above that.[3]

What does it mean to say that the "Social Security" portion of the payroll tax actually pays for Social Security benefits? Money is fungible, and nothing would change if the Social Security administrators swapped the cash from their share of payroll tax collections for the year for an equal amount of cash that had been raised through the income tax and initially shipped over to the Defense Department. In defense of the official characterization, however, the payroll tax was indeed first enacted in combination with introducing Social Security benefits, and legislation adjusting the tax has generally responded to changes in the current or expected future cost of providing the benefits. Moreover, as I further discuss in chapter 5, the government maintains a set of formal accounting entries called the Social Security Trust Fund that mainly compare Social Security tax receipts to benefit payouts under the theory that the former should pay for the latter. Social Security benefit checks cannot be issued in the absence of a positive Trust Fund balance without congressional authorization, thus making Trust Fund exhaustion a political trigger mechanism creating a need for legislative action.

Suppose we therefore accept that an 11.5 percent payroll tax up to the annual ceiling is indeed the "Social Security tax." This tax has various attributes that are worth noting. It applies only to observable wages (which need not, however, be paid in cash). Such forms of compensation as stock appreciation of a closely held corporation that results from its owners' work effort do not count, although many such returns to work might be over the annual ceiling anyway. Also, the Social Security tax does not apply to employee fringe benefits (such as employer-provided health care) that are excludable under the income tax. This omission may induce workers and employers to substitute these fringe benefits for straight salary even if they otherwise would have preferred to deal in cash (Steuerle and Bakija 1994, 169). And the Social Security system, including the tax, does not reach certain state and local government employees, providing them with a kind of tax preference in-sofar as they would lose from participating in the system.

The Social Security tax, if considered without regard to benefits, is highly regressive. It does not collect a penny more from someone who earns $10 million in a year than from someone who earns $80,000. No one can deny that people earning $10 million are materially much better off than those earning $80,000, all else equal, and are highly likely to feel less burden from paying the same dollar amount to the government. Nearly all of our taxes respond to this at least indirectly, but not the Social Secu-rity tax.

Two further features of the Social Security tax are worth noting before we turn to the benefit formula and its interactions with the tax. First, since its two-tiered rate structure of 11.5 percent and 0 applies on an annual basis (ig-noring certain peculiarities related to people with more than one employer), it hits people with "smooth" wage flows harder than people with "bouncy" wage flows. Suppose that Mark earns $150,000 from a single employer in Year 1 and nothing in Year 2, while Judy earns $75,000 both years. A tax of 11.5 percent on annual earnings up to $75,000 will force Mark to pay only $8,625 over the two-year period, while Judy will pay $17,250, or twice as much.

Second, the tax is paid purely on an individual, not a household, basis. Each worker pays tax up to the ceiling without regard to the taxes paid by spouses or other loved ones. Thus, suppose that spouses Ann and Bill earn a total of $150,000, as do spouses Carl and Dana, and that all four of these in-dividuals work. However, Ann earns $130,000 to Bill's $20,000 while Carl and Dana earn $75,000 each. Once again treating the Social Security tax as 11.5 percent on earnings up to $75,000 per individual, Ann and Bill pay a to-tal of only $10,925, whereas Carl and Dana pay $17,250.

Basics of the Social Security Benefit Formula

Poorly understood though the Social Security tax is (perhaps above all in workers' understanding of who bears the employer share), it stands as a stir-ring monument to clarity of public comprehension by comparison to the benefit formula. Perhaps not one worker in 100,000 really understands how a given increment of extra work will affect the value of his or her expected fu-ture benefits under present law. The widespread practice of illegal evasion, even and perhaps especially among low-wage workers to whom Social Secu-rity taxes and benefits may in the aggregate offer a net gain, may lend support to the suggestion by Laurence Kotlikoff and Jeffrey Sachs that "most contributors are likely to view the system's [11.5] percentage point payroll tax as a pure tax" (1997, 17).

Stupefying though the retirement benefit rules are, they are worth reviewing briefly. The next time someone asks you to explain the benefit formula at a cocktail party (admittedly, a remote contingency), you can smile inscrutably and say: "That's simple. Take the PIA on your AIME, adjust for your retirement age and spousal benefits, and then just index it." If they remain sufficiently interested to seek further amplification, you probably don't want to talk to them anyway.

A simplified version—incomplete and in some respects inaccurate, but close enough to understand most of the general issues discussed in this book—would go as follows: "The wage you used to earn is partly replaced by Social Security benefits. Up to a point, the more you used to earn, the more you get in absolute terms but the less you get as a percentage of your former earnings."

Readers who would find greater detail than this to be tedious should probably skip to the section, beginning at page 19, discussing the relationship between Social Security's tax and benefit rules. Only small portions of the rest of the book will be hard to understand if you do this. However, for those who would like further amplification, the following is a brief description of the benefit formula's main elements. After each, I comment briefly on its rationale and/or its incentive and distributional effects.

Relevant Career Earnings

To qualify for Social Security benefits, you must have worked during at least forty quarters (three-month periods). The "normal" retirement age for getting benefits is 65. You can elect to start up to three years early (age 62), but this comes at the price of permanently reducing your monthly benefit. You also can elect to start getting benefits up to five years late (age 70), in which case you receive compensation for the delay in the form of higher monthly benefits.

Under any of these retirement-age options, your monthly benefit depends on your average indexed monthly earnings (AIME). This is your average monthly wage for the best thirty-five years in your career. However, only covered earnings, or those subject to Social Security tax under then-applicable annual ceilings, are counted. And covered earnings from before you reached age 60 are indexed for both real and inflationary wage growth until you turned 60.[4] Years other than your top thirty-five are ignored for benefit purposes, and thus commonly are called your "dropout years."

Comment: The fact that retirement benefits depend on earnings makes the benefit portion of Social Security a wage subsidy. It increases what you get from working, just as a wage tax reduces what you get. However, this wage subsidy does not reach earnings above the annual ceiling (which at least were not subject to the Social Security tax) or from the dropout years (which were subject to it).

The disregard of noncovered earnings reduces the disparity in tax treatment between people with smooth versus bouncy annual wage paths. In terms of the earlier example, Judy has twice Mark's covered earnings for those two years as a result of paying twice the tax. Thus, she may end up with greater retirement benefits if all else is equal, although this may be inadequate compensation for paying more tax.

By contrast, the use of dropout years can increase the divergence between the tax treatment of people with smooth versus bouncy annual wage paths. Suppose two people have the same covered earnings and pay the same lifetime Social Security taxes, but that one had covered earnings only in his thirty-five best years, while the other earned less during these years but more in the dropout years. The first of these individuals, by reason of his bouncier wage path, has higher AIME and gets larger retirement benefits.

A powerful argument could be made that benefits should depend on people's entire work histories, not just their thirty-five best years. The basic claim is that while how much you earned during your entire career is an important datum for the government's distribution policy, the smooth versus lumpy pattern of your earnings lacks obvious significance.[5] Such a perspective might suggest eliminating the dropout years. However, this would tend to lower people's AIMEs, since your worst-earning years naturally reduce your average earnings. The change would therefore reduce Social Security payouts if the rest of the benefit formula remained the same. Yet the particular distributional hit that this change would impose has no logical connection to the case for using a fuller measure of career earnings. Its desirability therefore cannot be assumed even if you believe that, given Social Security's long-term financing problems, benefits have to be cut somehow.

Base Monthly Benefit

A second bit of jargon is the primary insurance amount (PIA). This is the basic monthly payment that Social Security will offer you (indexed for inflation) if you retire at age 65, and that is adjusted for early or late retirement. Accordingly, subject to these adjustments, it is the bottom line—the actual dollar amount on the check you get each month from Social Security. Your basic monthly benefit is a fraction of the AIME, computed via a three-bracket, declining-rate formula. You get 90 percent of your AIME up to a low dollar amount, 32 percent of your AIME from that point to an intermediate amount, and then 15 percent for remaining covered earnings.[6]

To give a sense of the formula's distributional effects, suppose you were born in 1937 and that your AIME is $1,250 ($15,000 per year). Your annual Social Security benefit (ignoring indexing for inflation between 1999 and 2002) comes out to $8,314.80. Triple your AIME to equal an annualized $45,000 per year, and your annual benefit does not quite double, increasing to $16,472.52.

Comment: The combination (with respect to covered earnings) of a flat-rate tax with a declining-rate benefit formula is the source of such progressive redistribution as Social Security accomplishes. However, the system's progressivity is reduced by the fact that benefits are not adjusted to reflect differences in life expectancy. The result is that members of long-lived groups do better than members of short-lived groups relative to what you would guess from just examining their PIAs. Examples of long-lived groups include high earners compared to low earners, women compared to men, whites compared to African Americans, and the college-educated compared to the non-college-educated.

The fact that high earners benefit financially under Social Security from living longer raises a possibility that the system actually is not progressive overall, as measured relative to lifetime income. However, most studies (such as Caldwell et al. 1999) find that it is modestly progressive on balance, although this depends on the discount rate that researchers use to measure the value to people in today's dollars of cash flows in the future. If you use a sufficiently high discount rate, the current system may actually appear regressive because "a higher discount rate reduces the present value of progressive benefits received during later retirement years by more than it reduces the present value of regressive taxes paid during earlier working years" (Coronado, Fullerton, and Glass 1999, 24).[7] The system would look more regressive still if you assumed that poorer people have a higher discount rate than richer people; that is, would require greater compensation in the form of interest to sacrifice money today in exchange for money in the future.

Retirement Age

Under rules applying through 2002, you get 100 percent of the PIA each month if you begin receiving benefits at age 65 (the "normal" retirement age). At present, the maximum annual benefit (ignoring spousal benefits, discussed below) is less than $20,000. You also have the option of retiring at age 62 and getting only 80 percent of the PIA from then on, or at age 67 or 70 and getting somewhat more than 100 percent. These benefit adjustments for early or late retirement are said to be roughly actuarially fair, in the sense of not greatly biasing the average participant's choice between the alternatives. After 2002 the normal retirement age will slowly increase until it reaches 67 in the year 2025.

Comment: The substantial increase in life expectancy since Social Security was introduced in the 1930s has prompted many to argue that the normal retirement age should go up (a kind of indexing to life expectancy). This would improve the system's long-term financing, since postponing the time when you begin receiving benefits under an unchanged formula reduces your total take. Increased life expectancy has played a large role in creating the current financing crisis. However, the fact that the normal retirement age is being increased so slowly may prompt a Red Queen phenomenon of running only in place (if that) so far as adjusting for life expectancy changes is concerned, since during the same time the average American life expectancy may well go up by more than two years.

Discouragement of Part-time Work

Between the ages of 62 and 70, if you elected to start receiving Social Security benefits but have earnings for the year in excess of a dollar ceiling, your benefits for the year are reduced. In 2002 beneficiaries between ages 62 and 65 will lose 50 cents of Social Security benefits for every dollar of earnings above an amount that will probably be about $11,000 (depending on wage level changes). Those between 65 and 70 will lose 33.3 cents of benefits for every dollar of earnings above $30,000. These benefit reductions are in effect marginal tax rates of 50 percent and 33.3 percent, respectively, which combine with income taxation and the like to reach overall levels that often range from 83 to 114 percent (Friedberg 1999, 2). The resulting work disincentive is reduced, however, by the fact that you can postpone Social Security retirement (and get higher annual benefits once it starts) if you anticipate having excess earnings during these years.

Comment: Social Security no longer induces retirement as strongly as it did before it was amended to reward postponing retirement through the allowance of increased annual benefits. But it still strongly discourages part-time work by people between the ages of 62 and 70 who have officially retired but don't want to stop working altogether. Subjecting these people to overall marginal tax rates that in some cases exceed 100 percent would appear to make little sense.[8] They may have much to contribute through work and may find that part-time work eases the difficult transition from work to retirement. Moreover, since their labor supply decisions tend to be highly tax-responsive, high earnings taxes on them may actually lose revenue in the aggregate.

Perhaps the best argument that has been advanced for taxing these individuals' part-time work at quite so steep a rate is that some may respond by choosing late retirement, and then be glad they have done so when the higher benefits help keep them out of dire poverty. Consider, for example, a widow who was a low earner due to her involvement in what economists call "home production," and who reaches the age of 70 with little in the way of savings. She may benefit when in her seventies from having been steered away from early retirement plus part-time work while in her sixties. Yet taxing part-time work is hardly the only (or most direct) way to induce her to choose late retirement or to increase her monthly benefits once she retires.

Income Taxation of Benefits

Under a maddeningly complex set of rules, Social Security benefits are excluded for income tax purposes by individuals with modified adjusted gross incomes below $25,000 ($32,000 for married couples). Above that point, the benefits are 50 percent includable, and the resulting income tax revenues officially attributed to the Social Security Trust Fund. The inclusion percentage rises to 85 percent for individuals with modified adjusted gross incomes above $34,000 ($44,000 for married couples), with the extra revenues from the increase in inclusion percentage being officially attributed to Medicare.

Comment: Republicans and Democrats have waged a series of comical struggles concerning whether increasing the income taxation of Social Security benefits is a "tax increase" or a "spending cut." The Democratic view is that it is a tax increase if President Reagan proposes it and a spending cut if President Clinton proposes it, while the Republicans maintain that the Democrats have it precisely backward. The dispute brings to mind the old *Saturday Night Live* gag, satirizing late-night TV commercials:

"It's a floor wax!"

"No, it's a dessert topping!"

"Floor wax!"

"Dessert topping!"

"Wait a second, it's both!"

Here, it truly is both, or equivalently neither, since the classification dispute is not economically meaningful. All that we can really say is that income tax inclusion of Social Security benefits increases people's lifetime net tax payment to the government.

Spousal Benefits

Social Security also provides spousal benefits, including but not limited to survivorship benefits. Once you reach age 65, you are entitled to 50 percent of your retired spouse's PIA (on top of his or her benefits) while he or she is alive, increasing to 100 percent after the spouse dies. However, you cannot receive both spousal benefits and your own benefits. Rather, you get whichever is higher, and the other is lost.[9] Minor dependent children of retirees also receive certain survivors' benefits.

Comment: Suppose you are working or considering work but are married to a higher-earning spouse. While your take-home earnings will be reduced by the Social Security tax, the benefits those earnings technically generate may be close to irrelevant given the likelihood that your spousal benefits will end up being higher. Insofar as you expect to claim spousal benefits in the end, Social Security bears on your work purely as a tax, not as a tax followed by an offsetting wage subsidy.

For this reason, Social Security's spousal benefit rules tend to discourage families' secondary earners, such as the wives of working husbands, from working. This is a group that tends to be highly responsive to taxes. The spousal benefit rules have therefore been strongly criticized for inducing greater economic dependence by married women on ongoing financial support from their husbands.

The flip side of the spousal benefit's discouraging work by secondary earners is its benefiting households in which only one spouse has worked. It therefore causes Social Security to transfer income from single to married households and from two-earner to one-earner married couples. The main motivation is apparently to aid widows who stayed home (for example, to raise children) during many or all of their working years, and who thus did not accrue significant Social Security benefits through their own participation in the system.

Notwithstanding such concerns, Social Security's effects in inducing would-be working wives to stay home and transferring wealth from two-earner to one-earner couples have become increasingly controversial. Even many commentators who generally are strong supporters of current Social Security consider them unacceptable and would therefore support altering the spousal rules even absent any fiscal pressure to change the system. As we will see, the issues posed are quite difficult, reflecting that for distribution policy generally (including, say, through the income tax or welfare system) the proper treatment of married and other households poses a set of unavoidable dilemmas.[10]

The Confusing Relationship between the Tax and Benefit Rules

Even without a long-term fiscal problem, the Social Security system plainly could be improved in many respects.[11] It could be viewed as two imperfectly integrated Rube Goldberg systems, one on the tax side and one on the benefit side. Neither the two sides in isolation nor their relationship is well understood by workers or voters. This has multiple implications, some clearly bad but others arguably good.

Many of the system's odd incentive and distributional effects reflect design elements, such as using dropout years and ignoring earnings above the annual ceiling, that may be largely administratively motivated. Any ill effects tend to be reduced, however, when the system at least mismeasures career earnings consistently on the tax and benefit sides. It helps, for example, that a worker with constant rather than variable earnings may both pay more taxes and receive more benefits. The especially dubious incentive and distributional effects of the spousal benefit rules reflect an unusual inconsistency between the two sides: Social Security taxes are levied purely on an individual basis yet benefits vary with marital status.

Even when the tax and benefit rules are roughly consistent, it matters that they are not directly calibrated to each other but run on separate tracks. Imagine for the moment that Social Security were a voluntary private retirement system, offered to subscribers by a private insurer. Tracking the relationship between contributions and the actuarial value of expected lifetime benefits would be essential to the success of the business. Customers would be hard to attract if one could not explain what they were paying and getting and why they should consider it a good deal. And if the insurer did not figure out a sensible way of relating contributions to benefits, it would be subject to bankruptcy if it guessed wrong, even apart from the perils of "adverse selection" if the customers it attracted were mainly those whose deal was too generous rather than too stingy.

The federal government is in a different position than a private insurer. It can overcome adverse selection by requiring everyone to subscribe. And it can pursue deliberate redistributive goals rather than needing to match contributions to expected benefits on an individual basis. Nonetheless, if there is one thing the government ought to care about as a feature of system operations, it is exactly how tax collections relate to expected benefit payouts for particular individuals and groups. Otherwise, the government risks not only blundering into awkward long-term financing problems, but failing to execute a coherent distributional policy or to give people sensible incentives. The confusing two-part structure of Social Security creates inherent difficulty in creating, tracking, and sustaining sensible tax-benefit relationships.

The structural disconnect between Social Security taxes and benefits may be convenient if you think that knowledge has a bad effect on political outcomes. Thus, suppose you consider yourself a wise policymaker who is unfortunately burdened with the need to placate a misguided voting public. You know that the general public thinks of Social Security as "a program in which the worker takes care of his own future, gets back at least what he has paid for, and is entitled to get it back as a right" (Derthick 1979, 289). Yet you also know that the public does not understand the fine points of the tax and benefit formulas or how they relate to each other.

Under these circumstances, having two imperfectly integrated systems to play with may greatly increase your freedom to do what you believe is right, without having to worry as much about public acceptance of your views. This consideration has indeed been crucial to Social Security's proponents throughout its history and, as Richard Nixon used to say of people he alleged were smearing him (although I mean it more sincerely), "I don't condemn them for it"—at least not unreservedly. Openness or policy transparency is an important value, but so is ending up with good policies, and the old debate about ends versus means has no fully satisfying answer.

The original rationale for muddying the relationship between Social Security taxes and benefits was to increase the potential to engage in hidden, but it was thought desirable, progressive redistribution. This was and is typically put in terms of giving the middle class a stake in government transfer programs if they are to be politically feasible; let the redistributive element stand alone and it will be politically vulnerable. To be effective, however, this requires not only combining multiple purposes within a single program, but obscuring the real relationship between these purposes.

A vague relationship between Social Security taxes and benefits was also originally convenient given the aim of providing benefits to the first post-enactment generation of retirees even though they had not significantly contributed to the system. This decision helped get votes for the program by promising what misleadingly looked like free money, but it may also have been good distributional policy. At least in some cases, it rescued needy retirees who found themselves without economic resources and opportunities after years of the Great Depression.

Keeping Social Security taxes and benefits so complex and unrelated may continue to aid the system's political backers today by helping to conceal real changes to the system, or at least making them seem smaller than they really are, by breaking them into multiple arcane parts. This was well demonstrated in a recent debate in the *Brookings Review* between privatization advocates Laurence Kotlikoff and Jeffrey Sachs on the one hand, and defender of the current system Henry Aaron on the other. Kotlikoff and Sachs argue that Social Security is currently so underfunded that, assuming no other changes, "we need to raise, immediately and permanently, the combined employer-employee OASDI payroll tax rate by 50 percent—from 12.4 [*sic*] percent to 18.4 percent—to avoid having to raise the tax rate by a much larger percentage down the road. This required 6 percentage point payroll tax hike is huge!" they conclude by way of more generally disparaging the current system (1997, 16).

Not so fast, Henry Aaron replies. The funding problem can be eliminated by taking six simple steps, such as adding five dropout years to the AIME (thus lowering average earnings and therefore benefits), reducing inflation adjustments, and raising the normal retirement age from 65 to 67 more swiftly than the law now mandates. Surely, Aaron concludes, the fiscal efficacy of such tinkering shows that "the air of crisis around Social Security is bogus" (1997, 17).

One might add: Aaron barely scratches the surface of how one could tinker with the benefit rules to improve the system's long-term solvency. Why not, for example, terminate wage indexing of one's past earnings for benefit purposes at age 55, rather than 60? What about shifting from wage indexing to mere inflation indexing of the rate brackets that are used to compute benefits?[12] Given five minutes, anyone who knows the basic rules should be able to come up with a dozen further changes that would be impenetrably obscure to most Americans yet improve Social Security's long-term financing. If all we care about is the arithmetical exercise of restoring the program's fiscal solvency, as distinct from examining what the changes would actually do, then all are equally good and there is no obvious limit to how much net revenue they can raise.

Kotlikoff and Sachs respond that, in substantial part, Aaron is merely proposing to replicate by disguised means the dramatic tax increase that they describe forthrightly. He is "chopping current workers' benefits [to the same effect as raising their taxes] by altering the benefit formula in ways they won't understand" and "giv[ing] workers a large dose of bad medicine in separate droppers" (1997, 23). The real difference between the 6 percentage point tax increase and this melange of seemingly technical changes is considerably smaller than the apparent difference.

To this, one who shared Aaron's political preference for the current system might reply: So much the better if the use of separate droppers helps as a political matter to prevent a shift to privatization that he argued would eliminate "America's best anti-poverty program . . . [place] risks on individual workers that they should not be expected to shoulder . . . [and] create costly and needless administrative burdens" (Aaron 1997, 17).

For another example of how Social Security's complex tax and benefit structure, coupled with its inducement to Clown family–like disregard of the overall picture, invites hiding the ball, consider the recent call by prominent Brookings Institution economist and former Congressional Budget Office chief Robert Reischauer, joined by a veritable *Who's Who* of leading Social Security experts, to close the system's long-term financing gap by "rais[ing] the Social Security tax ceiling on the American wage base to cover 90 percent of total earnings, instead of the current 86 percent" (Reischauer 1999, A-23).[13] Had Reischauer instead called the proposal by its true colors, as one to increase marginal tax rates by as much as 11.5 percent—assuming benefits would not also increase[14]—solely for a slice of earnings just above $72,000, it would have been not only politically untenable, but perhaps even abhorrent to some of those who advocated it. Reischauer, for example, has criticized flat tax proposals that would increase income tax liabilities in the range from $30,000 to $200,000, noting that "that's where most Americans are" (Shogan 1995, A-1). Apparently, then, tax policy is like designer clothing—you have to read the label to know what you think of a given policy effect.

I cannot say with confidence whether making Social Security policy more transparent would be good or bad overall. Let politicians and inside-the-Beltway policy entrepreneurs make that judgment. Yet clearer thinking about the system is indispensable at some stage in the reform process. Without it, you cannot tell whether the effects on Social Security policy of a given set of clever political tactics are indeed laudable.

Summary

The arbitrarily denominated "Social Security tax" applies to annual covered earnings at an 11.5 percent rate. Considered in isolation, this tax is quite regressive given its nonapplication to annual earnings above the ceiling. In addition, it can unduly penalize people whose career earnings paths were smooth rather than bouncy. Yet the system's net effect depends on the complicated relationship between Social Security taxes and benefits. Partly as a consequence of deliberate system design choices, this relationship is quite hard for workers and voters to understand.

The use of dropout years aside, the benefit formula applies to the same covered earnings as the tax, with a progressive payout scheme. It thus mitigates the tax's bias against smooth annual earnings and (considered without regard to life expectancy) more than negates the tax's seeming regressivity. The one case where it radically departs from roughly paralleling the tax—in providing spousal benefits even though taxes are levied purely on an individual basis—leads to substantial bias in favor of single-earner couples and against market work by the stay-at-home members of those couples.

The lack of any well-defined relationship between an individual's Social Security taxes paid and benefits received has various consequences even when the two schemes run on approximately parallel tracks. For example, it may cause many workers to overestimate the extent to which Social Security actually burdens their decisions to work. It can obscure the distributional effects of myriad tax and benefit changes. It complicates achieving a better measure of lifetime earnings (through elimination of the dropout years for AIME purposes) without simultaneously imposing a regressive one-time hit on workers who happen to be near retirement when such a change is adopted. And it encourages overlooking the effect on progressivity of providing benefits of greater actuarial value to people with longer life expectancies. While the specific policy of favoring people with longer life expectancies may be defensible—living longer increases your lifetime needs—it ought perhaps to receive greater scrutiny than is likely in a system where taxes and benefits run on separate tracks.

Any private insurer that was offering retirement annuities would need to price benefits against contributions on a more individualized basis. The government, since it can require universal worker participation in Social Security, has a power that private businesses lack to attempt redistribution through the program without inducing a run on the Treasury. Yet we cannot easily run a sensible distributional policy without having benefits received in some way directly depend on or relate to taxes paid. After all, the tax-benefit relationship determines what Social Security's distributional effects actually are. Perhaps the only good argument against reforming the system to make this relationship clearer (even if overall policy remains about the same) is that obfuscation promotes good political outcomes. This is possible but far from certain to be true.

3   Social Security as a System of Forced Saving and Limited Portfolio Choice Plus or Minus a Transfer

Why do people like the Social Security system so much and have such commitment to "saving" it? Perhaps the main reason is that they interpret the question "Should we save Social Security?" to mean "Should we or should we not give you money when you retire?" Thus interpreted, the question more or less answers itself.

One reason this question answers itself is that most of us prefer getting money to not getting money, all else equal. But people may especially like being assured of getting money after they retire because at that point they can easily imagine circumstances in which they would need it desperately. If you lose your job or go bankrupt at age 40 there is always hope, at least so long as you retain your health. Find yourself without resources at age 75 and you may really be sunk unless you have children who are willing and able to help you.

It is worth pausing to emphasize the distinction between these two reasons for Social Security's appeal. It looks like free money, due both to the lack of a clear or understandable link between its taxes and its benefits and to the pain of being caught in the middle if the system is scaled back just when you reach retirement age. (Once you retire, whatever you get really is free money.) Yet there is distinct appeal to the idea that, no matter how badly things go, you need not worry about utter destitution once you have become too old to work.

Both of these elements to the appeal of Social Security are worth addressing in turn. The first presents a case for replacing illusion with clear understanding. Nothing is free, including Social Security benefits, and understanding the system requires thinking about the tax-benefit relationship as it plays out for particular individuals. In the rest of this chapter, I go beyond the elementary point that there is no free lunch, to consider how we should think about the relationship between Social Security taxes and benefits.

The second element to the appeal of Social Security raises issues of social insurance that I discuss in chapter 4. What protections against economic risk ought our society offer to its members? Here Social Security is only a piece, although an important and in some ways distinctive one, of a much broader system and set of functions that often have not received the careful analysis they deserve.

Who Pays for What in Social Security?

Perhaps it is a bit unfair to suggest that people really think Social Security benefits are provided for free. After all, a typical paycheck openly discloses withholding for the worker's nominal share of the payroll tax. Nonetheless, Social Security's popularity as an "entitlement" begs the question: at least to the extent that you end up paying for your own benefits, does it make sense to think of them as an entitlement? If the government required you to go out to dinner once a week, would those dinners that you ate but also paid for (whether you wanted them or not) be "entitlements"?

The psychology of entitlement owes a lot to the perceived intergenerational character of the Social Security system. We are told that each generation of workers supports the generation that went before and is now retired. You become entitled by supporting the people who were retirees while you were working. Social Security therefore is merely the family writ large, with each generation both making and receiving gifts (albeit mandatory ones) that, ostensibly, only cold-blooded economists would describe as implicit exchanges or insurance rather than as acts of kindness.

What does it mean, however, to say that the benefits of a given group of retirees are paid for by current workers? Money is fungible; one dollar bill is no different than the next. Thus, it does not matter whether a given dollar of current payroll taxes actually is used to pay a given dollar of Social Security benefits, or even is placed in the bank account on which the benefit checks are written. Again, suppose that the Social Security Administration sent a billion dollars of Social Security tax revenues over to the Defense Department to buy weapons, and the Defense Department reciprocated by sending a billion dollars of income tax revenues (all received from elderly individuals) to pay for Social Security benefits. Would we now have transformed the Social Security system into one where the elderly, as a group, paid for their own benefits?

Since money is fungible, it never makes sense to say "*X* pays for *Y*" simply because of which dollar bills or even which bank accounts end up being used to pay for what. To be meaningful, the statement "*X* pays for *Y*" must depend on something further. When the same parties (such as U.S. citizens and the government) are engaged in multiple transactions, the answer to the question of who or what is paying for anything in particular depends on what you are trying to find out.

As it happens, there is a perspective from which it may make sense to say that current workers pay for current retirees' Social Security benefits. To dramatize the point through overstatement, suppose the U.S. Constitution mandated a strict annual "pay-as-you-go" retirement system in which retirees would by some formula divide an amount equal to the earmarked taxes that had been collected that year from workers under tax rules that Congress could set at its discretion. Under these conditions, the statement that "current workers pay for retirement benefits" might in a sense be true, no matter which actual dollar bills were used for what. It would be true if, notwithstanding the potential to make transfers outside the retirement system, the overall amount that retirees got depended on what workers were made to pay.

In actual fact, the Social Security system does not operate in quite this way. Possibly, however—depending on what Congress would actually do, or in the future actually does, under varying circumstances—it is like this to some extent. Social Security is considered a roughly pay-as-you-go system in which tax collections and benefit payments are supposed to be correlated with each other on something approaching an annual basis (although, in recent years, with increasing provision for a deliberate Trust Fund buildup). Accordingly, the statement "current workers pay for current retirees' benefits" might (although it is uncertain) make a plausible prediction about how some unexpected change to current Social Security tax collections would immediately affect benefit payments.

Yet the very same statement is unilluminating if you are inquiring into the Social Security system's effects over a given period of time in light of the tax and benefit rules for that period. What do I mean by the system's effects? A useful convention divides them into the "allocative" and the "distributional." "Allocative" refers to the mix of things that we collectively end up having, ranging from gold to houses to cars to uses of our own abilities and time. Here Social Security might, for example, affect how much people decide to work and save, as well as the investment assets they select for their personal portfolios. "Distributional" refers to who ends up with what share of all these various things. Here Social Security matters if it transfers lifetime resources from one individual to another.

To understand Social Security's allocative and distributional effects, the most informative way to answer the question "Who pays for the benefits?"

is to draw a distinction between oneself and everyone else—that is, self-payment versus receiving or making a transfer. Suppose that, in your own subjective terms, the cost of your lifetime Social Security taxes precisely equals the value of your lifetime Social Security benefits. Then, from a distributional standpoint, it makes sense to say that you paid for your own benefits and nothing but those benefits, wholly without regard to questions of which dollar bills were used for what. And from an allocative standpoint, your decisions along the way should not be affected (ignoring for now the significance of forced saving) if you think the system is having no net impact on you.

By contrast, if you get back either less or more than you contributed to the Social Security system, then it has a distributional impact on you. Moreover, if at any given decision point the system is operating either to your advantage or your disadvantage—for example, by paying a dollar of Social Security taxes you will earn extra benefits that you value either at 50 cents or at $1.50—then it is modifying your incentives. This raises at least the possibility that it will affect your decisions,[1] although this depends on how well you understand the system and how you actually make decisions.

In sum, there are at least three answers to the question "Who pays for Social Security benefits?" Payment in a literal sense might be said to depend on the exact details of cash flow but conveys no information of interest or value. Only by specifying an underlying inquiry, typically though a hypothetical question ("If such-and-so changed, what else would change?") can the payment question be made meaningful. The standard intergenerational answer ("Workers pay retirees' benefits") can illuminate questions of system design, and I occasionally use it in chapter 4, concerning social insurance, and chapter 5, concerning the Social Security Trust Fund. But the answer I use in the rest of this chapter, which is that people pay for their own benefits plus or minus a transfer, is in many ways the most informative. What makes it so is the prevalence of the distinction, in the minds of most people when they make decisions or experience greater or lesser personal well-being, between themselves (and perhaps close family members) and others.

A Simple Model of the Social Security System as Forced Saving Plus or Minus a Transfer

Social Security—including not just the current system but any likely to bear that name—has one key design feature. Under it, you pay taxes during your working years and receive benefits upon retirement. By contrast, under the sum of various income-based systems (such as the income tax, Temporary Assistance to Needy Families, and Food Stamps), the short-term cash flow between you and the government can go in either direction at any time in your life. This special design element to Social Security (which, as we will see in chapter 4, is crucial to evaluating its distinctive role in providing social insurance) also helps in conceptualizing its effects on people.

Given this design element, we can capture the essence of Social Security by starting with a very simple model. (There is plenty of time to add back real-world complexities as we go along.) Suppose initially that each individual's life consisted of just two moments and that there were no government programs except for Social Security. At Time 1, when the individual worked, he would pay a Social Security tax (T). At Time 2, when he was retired, he would receive a Social Security benefit (B).

If T equaled B, would this individual have broken even in his dealings with Social Security? The answer is no, because of the time value of money. In a world with positive interest rates, a dollar at Time 1 is generally more valuable than one at Time 2. In arm's-length transactions, less than a dollar needs to be lent at Time 1 to induce agreement to repay a dollar at Time 2. Or, starting with the loan of a dollar at Time 1, we would expect repayment of the dollar plus a positive return—call it r—at Time 2. We therefore need to know the relevant r in order to compare the value of T and B for a given individual.

In the real world, there is of course no single rate of return, even over a specified time period for which interest rates can be observed. For the moment, however, let's assume a single fixed r for comparing dollars at Time 1 to those at Time 2. This ostensibly is the return that all Time 1 loans (or other investments) yield and are known in advance to be certain to yield. In addition, assume that at this rate all individuals, given their total circumstances, are indifferent between borrowing and lending at Time 1. (They have already engaged in all the loan transactions that were needed to make them thus indifferent.)

Specifying r permits us to make meaningful statements about the Social Security system's effect on an individual notwithstanding the time lapse between Times 1 and 2. For example, suppose that you pay taxes of $10 and get benefits of $12. If r equals 20 percent, then in present value terms you precisely broke even from the system. But if r exceeds 20 percent you lost (your B was worth less in time-adjusted terms than your T), and if it is less than 20 percent you won (your B was more valuable than your T).

This, in turn, suggests that each individual's Social Security benefits (B) can be described as the sum of the following amounts: (1) T, or the Social Security taxes he paid, plus (2) r times T (henceforth, rT), or the return on these taxes paid—I still assume that there is one all-purpose interest rate—plus or minus (3) the extra amount that the system gives him or takes away from him. Let us call this amount "X" and describe it as the amount by which $T + rT$ needs to be adjusted in order to equal B. It is negative if the sum of $T + rT$ is greater than B.

We thus can use the following formula to describe Social Security's benefit payments to any individual:

$$B = T + rT + X.$$

This is a pure tautology. It holds in all cases simply because we define X as the amount needed to balance the equation. What makes it a useful tautology—a way of separating conceptually distinct elements in the system—is the fact that individuals, to the extent they can borrow and lend at r, should only care about X.

Bland and minimal though this basic description of Social Security may seem, it provides a powerful lens for examining the system's operations. Among other things, it helps to show that Social Security is really at least two separate programs wrapped together. First, it is a system of forced saving, insofar as it requires workers to contribute T today in exchange for B in the future, or at the least to defer receiving B although it presumably has a present value today.[2] Second, it is a redistributive program insofar as it shifts resources from people with a negative X to those with a positive X. Each of these programs merits further discussion.

Social Security as Forced Saving

The forced saving component of Social Security is easy to misunderstand. What the system unmistakably does is require a certain level of saving: (a) through the system but not necessarily overall, (b) by a given individual but not necessarily by society as a whole. Each of those two components is more complicated than it may initially seem.

The sense in which a given individual is forced to save "through the system" is quite specific. Ignoring for the moment all other financial transactions that you might engage in, its sequence of cash flows reduces the money you have available to spend on consumption today and increases the money you will have available to spend on consumption in the future. Indeed, even if you pay no tax and just get a B that was entirely funded by a transfer, your lifetime consumption opportunities are being deferred (absent offsetting transactions) relative to the case where you got a transfer of the same present value immediately.

This deferral of consumption to the future is exactly what "saving" means. Yet Social Security's true net effect on your consumption path is harder to gauge. For example, the apparent forced saving through the system is utterly irrelevant if, as I have assumed for convenience so far, you can freely borrow and lend at r, and indeed use this ability to pursue self-selected savings targets without regard to the system's cash flows.

The sense in which Social Security need not result in forced saving by the society as a whole, even if it does induce forced saving by a given beneficiary, can be illustrated through a simple hypothetical. Suppose we have a two-person society, composed of Bob and Carol. Without any need to work, they each receive manna from the sky, which they can eat now or save for later. Bob, however, always eats immediately whatever manna he has on hand. If Carol takes some of Bob's manna today in exchange for manna in the future, Bob is being forced to save. Yet there need not be any overall saving, since Carol can eat this manna plus all of her own. In that case, she would be offsetting Bob's saving through her own dissaving. Society as a whole would be saving zero, just as it would be if both individuals ate all of their own manna. The program would still be significant, however (unlike in the case where the worker's own consumption is not actually shifted), because it would shift Bob's consumption from the present to the future and Carol's from the future to the present.

The analogy between this hypothetical and the actual Social Security system is quite close if we assume that collecting Social Security taxes causes government spending on current consumption to increase by precisely the same amount that paying the taxes causes workers' current consumption to decline. In practice, the extent of this offset depends on the relative marginal propensities to save of the worker versus whoever determines how the government funds are used. Some prominent analysts, such as Martin Feldstein and Laurence Kotlikoff, argue that Social Security actually *reduces* national saving, by transferring money from people more inclined to save (workers) to those more inclined to consume (retirees). The point for now, however, is not to insist on any particular conclusion regarding Social Security's effect on national saving, but simply to note the distinction between how it affects saving by a particular worker and by society as a whole.

To the extent that Social Security forces an individual to save, it may reduce the value he assigns to B relative to T. The result could be what economists call deadweight loss—in effect, a negative adjustment to X for this person, unaccompanied by a positive adjustment to X for anyone else. (Chapter 4 discusses what policy considerations might motivate imposing this apparent loss.) Other respects in which Social Security, as described so far, could induce deadweight loss pertain to people's labor supply responses to its effect on work incentives and to its administrative costs, if greater than those that these individuals would incur in its absence through increased use of private retirement plans providing similar services.

Social Security as a Redistributive Program

To the extent that Social Security is a redistributive rather than a forced saving program, it transfers wealth from some workers to others. Stated in terms of lifetime earnings, it provides a *net wage tax* to those who lose from it and a *net wage subsidy* to those who gain from it. Social Security therefore has straightforward distributional effects (some people win from it and others lose). It also has allocative effects, such as on people's work decisions, that may need brief elaboration.

One way in which Social Security transfers can affect work and other allocative decisions is through its income effects, which arise when a change in your economic well-being alters your willingness to work. A good illustration is Michael Jordan's decision in 1998 to retire from professional basketball even though he could have earned $34 million by playing for one more year. If Jordan had suddenly lost all his wealth and had no other way of getting it back, this opportunity would surely have become more appealing to him.

Social Security transfers can also affect labor supply through incentive effects. A real-world example would be a decision by a woman with a working husband to stay home because available jobs do not offer her enough money after paying the Social Security tax (which is purely a tax if she expects to end up with spousal benefits). Even many fervent supporters of the current Social Security system agree that the resulting effect on married women's work decisions is both significant and undesirable, and they have been exploring various ways in which it could be mitigated without unduly cutting spousal benefits for widows (Aaron and Reischauer 1998, 96–100).

One further clarification about Social Security's allocative effects may be in order. Distributionally, what matters the most is the system's actual material effect on different individuals. Allocatively, however, people's perceptions may be more important than the reality. After all, I can only base my work decisions on what I believe to be true. This is where the Kotlikoff-Sachs argument—that people may fail to understand that Social Security retirement benefits (considered apart from the tax) are a wage subsidy—

becomes important. If "most contributors . . . view the system's . . . payroll tax as a pure tax" (Kotlikoff and Sachs 1997, 17), then it is discouraging work, along with voluntary compliance with the payroll tax, to a greater extent than it would if correctly understood. If Kotlikoff and Sachs are correct, even without a policy change, therefore, somehow making the wage subsidy more transparent or better understood would reduce inefficient tax deterrence of work.

The Limited Number of Mechanisms for Increasing Social Security Benefits

Suppose we want to increase Social Security retirement benefits (B) for a given individual. This can be done in only three ways. The first is to increase his taxes (T), thus increasing his forced saving (barring other adjustments) so that he will pay for the extra retirement benefits himself. The second is to increase the actual investment return, or rT, that is earned on his tax payment. I defer discussing this possibility for the moment, because I am still assuming that there is only one fixed rate of return in the economy. The third is to make a positive change to his transfer from the system (X), including by moving it closer to zero if it is presently negative. This means that, relative to the preceding state of affairs, we are making a transfer to this individual from someone else.

In the real world, with its multiple tax and transfer systems, there are also Clown family accounting versions of these changes. For example, suppose we increase my T so that I can self-finance increased B, but that we describe this as an increase in my income taxes to finance increased Social Security benefits. Now, while I am still paying for my increased retirement benefits, a computation of T and B that was limited to Social Security would misleadingly suggest that only B had changed, thus inviting the false implication that I was doing better than previously. In short, we might have "saved Social Security" for me without actually aiding me except insofar as I benefited from the extra forced saving.

Now suppose instead that other people bear the increased future income tax liability. A comprehensive view would show increases in their T's and my B, along with a transfer that would be depicted as negative X to them and offsetting positive X to me. A Clown family accounting version that looked only at Social Security would ignore the adverse changes for them and show only the favorable changes for me. Once again, we would have "saved Social Security" to no good end, so far as overall social policy was concerned, unless it happened to be good policy for the adversely affected individuals to pay me transfers via an increased retirement pension.

As it happens, Social Security at present is subject to one pervasive complaint apart from the prospect that its long-term financing may collapse. This is the complaint that, even assuming all current promises are kept, it does not offer current or future workers a good enough deal. Under most estimates, "internal rates of return" from the system—a computation of the r that would be needed to equalize B with $T + rT$ if X were dropped from the equation—are low already and dropping fast for succeeding generations. According to Caldwell et al., Social Security offers an average internal rate of return of 2.4 percent for people born in 1945–49, dropping below 1 percent for people born after 1965, and approaching zero for people born after 1995 (1999, table 9). The last group, therefore, would barely get back what they put in, making the program akin to a mandatory zero-interest long-term savings account or to a program that transferred about 80 percent of their tax contributions to members of older generations and then invested the remaining 20 percent at a market interest rate (4). The effect on younger participants would look worse still if we also considered, as Caldwell et al. for computational convenience do not, the income taxation of Social Security benefits.

One problem with using "internal rates of return" to analyze Social Security's effects on various groups is that it may lead you to confuse what I call r with what I call X. That is, it encourages you to think of the program as if it were a mutual fund that was consistently failing to achieve a competitive return, presumably because the fund managers were picking the wrong investments. This is an error, at least in emphasis, insofar as the real issue is that Social Security has been a vehicle for making intergenerational transfers. Younger generations' overall fortunes, both within the contours of Social Security and more generally, cannot help but be affected by the decision to hand a large portion of their contributions (in terms of real value, not just the details of cash flow) to older generations.

This transfer may have been good or bad policy (I discuss it further in chapter 4), but should in any event be correctly understood. And once a transfer has become irrevocable, in that its recipients are either dead, politically entrenched, or inspire too much sympathy (like retirees with no other assets) for us to want to target them, there is nothing further to be done about it. The fact that some of your Social Security taxes may have been paid to someone else has no direct bearing—as internal rate of return analysis would seem to imply—on what investment strategy you should follow as to the rest.[3] Nonetheless, the issues buried in the term I call r, arising from the fact that there is no single invariant rate of return in our economy, merit some scrutiny, and I turn to them next.

Varying or Unclear Interest Rates

Again, the time lag between paying Social Security taxes and receiving retirement benefits matters due to the time value of money: the fact that a dollar today is generally worth more than a dollar in the future, because you can invest it today at a positive interest rate and expect to receive more than a dollar in the future. So far in this chapter, I have simplified the analysis by assuming a single invariant interest rate that applies to all possible trades between present and future money. This assumption is of course false. Indeed, if it were true, a program of forced saving might be completely vacuous. Anyone who didn't like paying T as a worker in exchange for $T + rT$ as a retiree could completely undo the program's effect on when he consumed by arranging a side transaction whereby he borrowed T during his working years and repaid $T + rT$ at retirement.

If I am liquidity-constrained, in that I cannot borrow today against a given expectation of money in the future, then r is essentially a subjective term describing my preferences. At what interest rate would I be willing to borrow against this expectation, and thus what is its smaller or discounted present value to me today? Such a computation would be needed to determine both Social Security's distributional effect on me and its influence on my work and other incentives.

Obviously, people who are liquidity-constrained may vary in their regret about being so. Poorer people in particular may tend both to be more liquidity-constrained and to discount future benefits more steeply than other individuals. Evidence that this is so can perhaps be deduced from studies of life-cycle saving patterns, which suggest that people with lower lifetime earnings generally save a lower percentage of what they have (Lawrance 1991). The conclusion that liquidity-constrained poor workers have a relatively high subjective discount rate for retirement benefits would make the Social Security system appear less progressive than otherwise, unless we concluded that they were mismeasuring their own well-being on a lifetime basis.

Most empirical studies that try to measure Social Security's distributional effects apply the same discount rate to everyone. What rate to use, however, has proven highly controversial. The discount rates in prominent recent studies range from 2 percent (Steuerle and Bakija 1994) to 7 percent (one of the alternatives in Caldwell et al. 1999). Just to show how much this matters given the miracle of compound interest, $100 in thirty years is worth $55.21 today at a 2 percent discount rate but only $13.14 at a 7 percent discount rate. Thus, the varying assumptions have an enormous effect on what the studies find. The degree of burden that Social Security places on younger compared to older generations, the system's likely fiscal sustainability over time, and the extent of its progressivity within an age group all vary enormously depending on the discount rate that you use in making computations.

The difficulty of determining the right discount rate goes beyond the fact that interest rates frequently change or that subjective discount rates are hard to observe. In addition, observed market interest rates require interpretation because they amalgamate a variety of distinct components that have varying significance. Among the possible components of an observed interest rate are the following:

- A service fee to financial institutions that serve as intermediaries in the flow of funds from ultimate lenders to ultimate borrowers. Banks would be unable to demand more interest on loans than they offer on deposits if the services they provide were not costly to them and valuable to their customers. This element of compensation for services is generally thought distinct from interest as such (it could, for example, take the form of a separate fixed charge), and discount rates thus generally leave it out.

- Compensation by borrowers for money's expected loss of purchasing power over time due to inflation. Only "real" or inflation-adjusted interest provides a positive return to lenders, and thus should be reflected in r.

- A risk premium insofar as an expected investment return is subject to variance. Almost no investment is entirely risk-free, but the expected return that investors demand generally increases with the expected variance. Questions of risk have been emerging as central to the Social Security debate. For example, they underlie the debate concerning whether Social Security tax revenues should, in one way or another, be invested in the stock market. They therefore merit fuller consideration next.

The Risk-Return Frontier

An investor who chooses a safe investment in lieu of a riskier one that offers a higher expected return is deliberately turning his back on expected wealth. Yet no irrationality is thereby implied. Risk aversion is simply an investor preference, and indeed one that is easy to rationalize in terms of the declining marginal utility of money as you get wealthier. If you satisfy your most urgent needs first, then each extra dollar may provide you with less subjective benefit than the one before. Thus, you may reasonably be reluctant to bet, say, $10,000 on the toss of a coin that is slightly biased in your favor. Risk aversion is what makes insurance a profitable business. You may be happy, for example, to increase your expected cost of driving a car in exchange for making the downside (from an accident) less dire.

Since time only moves forward and there are no replays, each investment ultimately has an outcome that may be above or below some notional expected return. Nonetheless, it is convenient to think of risk-averse investors as balancing expected return against perceived risk when they make investment decisions. The greater the variance in expected outcomes, the greater the mean expected return must be to attract such investors. An investment that offers too little return for the risk, or too much risk for the return, stands to be less appealing than the alternatives.

Accordingly, the investments that might be appealing under prevailing market conditions can in principle be plotted across what economists call the *risk-return frontier*. This might take the visual form of a graph with risk on the horizontal axis and return on the vertical axis. The "frontier" is the line drawn by connecting the points that showed the necessary (and continually increasing) return at each increasing risk level.

Returns above the risk-return frontier constitute special opportunities that should get snapped up by those with access to them, without becoming generally available. An example might be Bill Gates's early stake in Microsoft, if he was not just extremely lucky but bound, on average, to do exceptionally well given his entrepreneurial abilities and inside information about them. Returns below the frontier are bad investments that you ought not to make in your own self-interest unless making a particular one is fun, like betting at the casino (or perhaps participating in an Internet start-up). Needless to say, there are enough ill-informed or irrational investors in the world for bad investments often to be made without this recreational element. A good example is the recent case where investors in Albania, handicapped by their inexperience, suffered massive losses from investing in fraudulent Ponzi schemes that purported to offer 50 percent a month but in fact evaporated almost immediately (Friedman 1997).

Returns right at the risk-return frontier are equal in the eyes of the market. Thus, if 2 percent is the riskless rate and 8 percent the rate at a given risk level, then a riskless asset paying $2 per year and an asset at that risk level paying $8 per year are each worth $100. People with ready access to well-functioning capital markets can swap one for the other at any time. Thus, you have not inherently pulled off a coup of any sort if you increase your expected yield by trading low-risk for high-risk assets that both lie along the risk-return frontier. This is a point that advocates of at least notionally "investing" some portion of Social Security tax revenues in the stock market often overlook.

Nonetheless, investors need not be indifferent between assets at different points along the risk-return frontier, just as they might prefer one food to another that sells for the same price. One reason for their differing preferences is factual ambiguity. Real-world investments tend not to come with labels that provide authoritative statements of the true expected return and risk level for what will, in the end, be a one-time event. People may thus disagree about where particular investment opportunities actually lie relative to the notional frontier.

Even assuming certainty about the odds, however, people with different risk preferences may want to locate their overall investment positions at different points along the frontier. Moreover, in practice they may want to hold a particular mix of assets that lie at different points along the risk-return frontier. Thus, given the rest of your positions, you may actually prefer Asset A to Asset B, where each has the same market value but they lie at different points along the risk-return frontier.

If you were forced to trade Asset A for Asset B and for some reason could not readjust your overall holdings, you presumably would consider yourself worse off despite the unchanged market value. You might, however, be expected to eliminate this subjective loss by moving back to the point you preferred, so long as you had consistent risk preferences, knew what you were doing, and did not face significant transaction costs. If the government requires you to hold a given asset, whether by direct regulation or actually holding it on your behalf, you should be indifferent as to whether this asset is A or B if you can and do adjust your overall holdings to end up where you prefer. The government's asset choice on your behalf is significant only insofar as market frictions or a lack of consistent risk-regarding behavior on your part prevents seamless readjustment.

The existence of multiple assets that have varying risk and return characteristics, and that involve distinct bets about the resolution of different uncertainties, gives rise to an important element in saving decisions that I ignored in the earlier discussion predicated on a single rate of return. Savers in a world with multiple investment opportunities can exercise *portfolio choice*.

That is, they can choose particular combinations of expected risks and returns, and decide which bets are actually worth making given their own personal preferences and estimates of the odds. If you can borrow, the opportunity to engage in portfolio choice is not limited to your net saving.

Risk versus Return in Social Security

We now can evaluate how the general relationship between expected returns, risks, and market or subjective value bears on Social Security. This evaluation is best performed in two stages. First, I assume that the current rules specifying Social Security taxes and benefits (including future changes that are already scheduled to occur) are guaranteed to remain in force forever, notwithstanding the vagaries of politics and the system's financing problems. While this assumption is quite unrealistic, such stability is arguably an ideal of the current system, and thus something that its supporters would like to achieve once they had restored Social Security's long-term solvency. Second, I consider how the analysis changes once we take into account the system's political and financing risks.

For any given worker, the current Social Security rules provide approximately determinate answers to the question of what will be your net wage tax or subsidy if you have a particular wage path and life span.[4] The passage of time increasingly resolves any wage uncertainty and causes your Social Security tax to lie in the past. Thus, upon retirement you are left with an asset, having the value of your expected lifetime Social Security benefits. In real annual terms (ignoring uncertain life expectancy), this asset offers a fixed or risk-free return. Unlike corporate stock, its payout is not tied to the performance of a given company or the economy. Unlike many bonds or private annuities, the payout is indexed for inflation and comes from an issuer (the U.S. government) that faces virtually no prospect of involuntary default. Even the implicit "bet" on longevity, since by living longer you receive more benefits, is a hedge against the risk of increasing your lifetime needs by living longer.

By offering only a particular fixed payout scheme, Social Security establishes its third key characteristic beyond forced saving and redistribution. This is denying portfolio choice to participants, at least within the system's formal confines. Only one type of payout is available. In addition, participants are required to make the longevity bet even if they would prefer a fixed asset value that they could invest as they chose upon retirement (or sooner) or bequeath to their heirs if they died before retirement.[5] As in the case of forced saving through Social Security, the limit on portfolio choice applies, if at all, to a given participant. It has no necessary implications for what real investments, with what tradeoffs between risk and expected return, are being made by the society as a whole.

The fixed character of Social Security benefits (life expectancy aside) makes them more valuable than a cash flow of the same expected amounts that is subject to greater variance. Yet an investor who prefers a riskier, higher-yielding point along the risk-return frontier will regret being unable (if he is unable) to hold such an asset in lieu of what Social Security offers. As between two assets (the actual one and the riskier one) that might both be life annuities[6] having the same market value, he may end up with the one he values less. Ignoring for now the possible arguments (discussed in chapter 4) for overriding the investor's preference, this creates deadweight loss, in much the same manner as paying to give people food that they do not like.

Whether investors actually are, in the end, affected in this manner by Social Security's denial of portfolio choice depends on how, if at all, they adjust the rest of their portfolios. The adjustments you can make include holding riskier assets outside the system than you would otherwise have selected, perhaps financed by low-risk borrowing that offsets Social Security's low-risk yield. Such adjustments can eliminate the bottom-line effects of the system's apparently denying portfolio choice with respect to its benefits.

One problem I have so far ignored, however, is that future Social Security benefits are not in fact risk-free. Supporters of the current system may aspire to creating certainty about retirement support but cannot hope to do so in full. Social Security participants are subject to two types of risk with respect to their involvement in the system. The first is a risk of political change. Neither Social Security taxes or benefits are constitutionally set in stone. They do not even have the legal status of binding debt obligations. This makes the tax and benefit levels potentially fair game, just like everything else within the ambit of possible political change, for anyone with political influence who wants to change them. To be sure, the same holds for all potentially taxable investment returns from ostensibly risk-free assets. Yet Social Security benefits may conceivably be deemed riskier than the interest return on government bonds even though the taxation of the latter could change.

Second, Social Security faces unavoidable financing risks. Over time, it is supposed to be self-financing. However, even if it were not artificially separated from the rest of the government's budget, it would share in a broader set of financing risks given that all government spending must eventually be paid for by someone. One simply cannot command a set of preset tax and spending rules to remain in fiscal equipoise over time, any more than King

Canute could command the tide to stop rising. The financing risk includes the possibility that, say, your future income tax burden may vary depending on Social Security's financing needs.

We thus cannot make Social Security a truly risk-free system in anything beyond a Clown family accounting sense (where financing risk is simply shunted outside the system's official boundaries but remains a real problem for participants). And given the difficulty of predicting the future, this is a significant problem. Just in Social Security's first fifty years, shifting economic and demographic trends twice radically altered its long-term prospects. In the 1930s President Roosevelt was told that it stood to face serious revenue shortfalls within thirty years—a projection he suppressed (Achenbaum 1986, 20, 28, 32) but that proved mistaken due to unforeseen economic expansion. Then beginning in the late 1970s, emerging trends such as slower productivity growth, increased life expectancies, and the baby bust that followed the post–World War II baby boom brought about a period when its estimated long-term fiscal picture kept worsening.

Admittedly, we can absolve the members of a particular group, such as current retirees, from bearing upside or downside risk. Indeed, international evidence from a range of major industrial nations with social security systems suggests that downside financing risks are largely borne by young and middle-aged workers, rather than by retirees and near-retirees (McHale 1999). For the population as a whole, however, running a social security program cannot help but be a risky proposition.

More on Social Security's Financing Risks

Political and financing risk would reduce the discounted value of Social Security benefits even if the risk of change were symmetric, in the sense that gain and loss relative to the current rules were equally likely. However, these risks do not alter Social Security's denial of portfolio choice. Participants who cannot make outside adjustments to their portfolios still end up getting amounts determined by a uniform, one-size-fits-all benefit formula. They can neither opt out of Social Security's political and financing risks by accepting some enforceable commitment to receive a particular benefit stream nor elect through the system to bear other risks that might increase their expected returns.

Making things worse for today's workers, Social Security's current political and financing risks are not symmetric. The system's long-term financing problems suggest that things are likely to change for the worse so far as current and future generations are concerned. Indeed, the change in mean expected outcome might be substantial. According to some estimates, restoring Social Security's long-term fiscal balance would require an immediate 50 percent increase in its taxes (Kotlikoff and Sachs 1997, 16) or else an immediate 25 percent reduction in its benefits (Ferrara and Tanner 1998, 52).[7]

While these two alternative routes to restoring fiscal balance may look quite different—one is called a "tax increase" while the other is called a "spending cut"—in some respects they are similar. To be sure, they might have very different distributional impacts upon adoption given where different participants stand in their life cycles. (Current retirees are unaffected by a Social Security tax increase.) Yet either change would increase the net wage tax that Social Security levies on affected participants over their lifetimes. To the extent that a given participant would lose the same amount from either (depicted in my basic formula as an increase in X), the main difference between them is that a tax increase implies greater forced saving than a benefit cut. It increases your payout during your working years, rather than reducing what you get back upon retirement.

What are the broader implications of Social Security's political and financing risks? Obviously, risks of random change, such as where different groups successively win temporary control of Congress and alter the rules in their favor, are undesirable even without regard to the resulting creation of incentives to waste resources engaging in a political arms race. However, one cannot evaluate political risk without taking into account the possibility that the changes will on average be improvements, at least in the sense of adapting to changing conditions and new information (Shaviro 2000). So far as financing risks are concerned, once the expected direction of change has become clear, there is a case for reducing uncertainty by letting people know as soon as possible just how their net wage taxes are going to be increased (Shaviro 1997a, 309). One might as well take today, rather than postpone, the step of establishing a sustainable long-term policy course, both to aid people's planning and to comfort the risk-averse.

This is not to say, however, that making Social Security as fixed a system as possible would be desirable even if all participants were highly and equally risk-averse. Under some circumstances, exposure to a given risk can add certainty to your overall position because it offsets other risks that you cannot avoid bearing. In illustration, it is hard to think of a riskier investment on the upside, so far as isolated asset payoffs are concerned, than buying car insurance. After all, you might lose your bet by having no accidents and thus getting nothing. Or you might instead win a million dollar payoff by having a really big accident that would otherwise cost you a million dollars. What makes your coverage a form of insurance, rather than a speculative bet against your own driving ability, is its correlation with the bet in favor of your driving abilities that you unavoidably make each time you get on the road.

The question of risk in Social Security therefore brings us to the fundamental social insurance issues that underlie our entire tax-transfer system. Why does Social Security redistribute wealth, try to require saving, and try to limit portfolio choice? What considerations should affect the provision of social insurance? What roles can and should a retirement system such as Social Security play in helping to provide such insurance?

Summary

The rhetoric of "entitlement" that we use to describe Social Security benefits should not obscure the fact that someone must pay for them. They are best viewed as representing forced saving by the recipient, plus or minus a transfer to or from other participants. A third key Social Security feature, in addition to forced saving and redistributive transfers, is denial of portfolio choice within the system. You are subject to the system's political and financing risks but cannot select the particular features (such as a given tradeoff between risk and expected return) that you would like.

Both the forced saving and the limit on portfolio choice can be reversed by a participant who responds by altering his other decisions—for example, by dissaving outside the system and borrowing to hold risky assets. In addition, these features need not imply increased or less risky saving by the society as a whole. After all, a commitment to pay a given dollar of Social Security benefits is not a net asset of the society, but rather an asset to one person and a liability to someone else.

Social Security's redistributive transfers are not similarly reversible through the exercise of individual choice. These transfers, while often obscured from view by the rhetoric of entitlement, are largely responsible for the system's offering such meager internal rates of return to participants born after World War II. Giving some of your money to someone else naturally reduces your overall return. Yet a focus on overall returns may lead people mistakenly to conclude that the part they got back must have been mishandled, rather than that they have paid net wage taxes through Social Security to finance other people's net wage subsidies.

As a historical matter, the net wage subsidy to early generations of Social Security participants required subsequent generations to pay a net wage tax. Most estimates suggest, however, that the net wage tax already scheduled through the tax and benefit rules on the books will not prove large enough to meet expected financing needs. Net wage taxes may therefore have to be increased, whether through tax increases or benefit cuts. These two alternatives differ in two main respects: only a benefit cut reaches current retirees, and a tax increase implies greater forced saving than a benefit cut if you would lose equally from both.

4   Social Security and Social Insurance

Private Insurance and the Circumstances Where Government Action Extending It May Be Desirable

Before evaluating Social Security's role in providing social insurance, we need to consider what "social insurance" is and why one might find it appealing. This suggests briefly considering private insurance, such as the fire, theft, automobile, and health policies that you might want, or even be required, to purchase from a commercial provider.

Ambrose Bierce gave the cynic's definition of insurance, calling it an "ingenious modern game of chance in which the player is permitted to enjoy the comfortable conviction that he is beating the man who keeps the table" (Bierce 1993 ed., 63). This would indeed be the explanation if the highly variable outcomes of the "bets" it involves—as when you either win thousands of dollars from the automobile insurance company to defray the cost of a highway smashup, or else your policy proves a dud by paying nothing—stood alone, rather than offsetting other undesired bets that your circumstances caused you to make.

Given the offset to these other bets, however, people often willingly accept a negative return from insurance in the form of a premium that exceeds the expected payoff and consider this simply the price of receiving a valued service. A negative-return insurance bet that reduces the overall variation to which you are subject can increase your expected utility or satisfaction despite reducing your expected income. This, again, reflects declining marginal utility, or the tendency of each additional dollar to be worth less to you than the dollar before since you satisfy your most urgent needs first.

What is in it for the insurance company? In a competitive market, the price it can charge merely covers its transactions costs, such as handling paperwork, sending out an appraiser to assess damage, and earning a normal return on capital (Barr 1993, 117). To be sure, markets are not always perfectly

44

competitive. Nonetheless, what fundamentally permits the insurance business to go forward is the law of large numbers. Even if one person's driving or health outcomes are hard to predict in advance, those of a large group operating independently under known conditions may be highly predictable. Similarly, while a single coin toss will come out either 100 percent heads or 100 percent tails, a million tosses of an honest coin are virtually certain to come out very close to 50-50.

Since pooling together lots of separately resolved risks is the fundamental insurance "trick," it often is made part of the basic definition of insurance, as Robert Shiller explains: "The function of insurance is to allow people to escape risks that are concentrated on them and to share these risks over large numbers of people. Management of risks does not make the risks disappear, instead they are spread over many people so that their effects are less painful" (1998, 1). One should distinguish, however, between (a) insurance's fundamental objective of protecting people against risk and (b) a specific method, such as risk-spreading and the use of actuarial group forecasts, by which that objective might be pursued. "Even where institutions are not insurance in the sense of (b), they might still be regarded as insurance in that they offer protection against risk" (Barr 1993, 111). This distinction between the aim of managing risk and the methods typically used by commercial insurers will prove important in evaluating how Social Security can help provide social insurance.

People face an enormous variety of risks in their lives that might make insurance attractive. Consider the possibility that your house will lose value or your job disappear due to broader economic factors. Private insurance markets nonetheless are quite incomplete; they cover only a handful of discrete, fairly dramatic risks such as those of dying, getting sick or injured, being sued, and losing property in a fire. In part, this may reflect psychological barriers to people's appreciating the benefits of novel forms of risk mitigation, as has arguably been evidenced by the frequent failure in the marketplace of innovative financial products that hedge various seemingly undesirable risks (Shiller 1993, 17). Yet the standard transaction whereby a private firm offers insurance coverage for a premium faces a number of potential obstacles even if consumers are potentially eager to subscribe, in particular:

- Insured losses must be reasonably measurable and (to counter fraudulent claims) verifiable. One could not offer insurance, say, against having a bad meal, even if people wanted the insurance, unless one could devise a decent measure of meal quality.

- People must be able to enter into insurance contracts before the underlying uncertainties are resolved. Thus, getting health insurance is quite a different proposition after you test positive for the AIDS virus than before.

- The insurer must be able to mitigate problems of *adverse selection*, which arise when the prospective purchasers of insurance have superior information about their own risks. Thus, suppose that there are low-risk and high-risk individuals who know their own identities but whom the insurance company cannot tell apart. Any effort to offer insurance to low-risk individuals at a reasonable rate (given their actual expected losses) will induce relative oversubscription by the high-risk individuals who know that at these odds they are indeed beating the man who keeps the table. The result may be that no one can be insured for a premium that is set below the high-risk individuals' expected loss.

- The insurer must be able to mitigate problems of *moral hazard*, which arise when it cannot perfectly monitor actions by insured individuals that affect the occurrence or magnitude of a covered loss. An example would be driving too fast or under the effects of alcohol because you know that the company will pay your accident costs if you crash. Insurers have a number of tools for addressing moral hazard. For example, they may impose deductibles that deny coverage for a fixed dollar amount, along with coinsurance that requires the insured to bear a specified percentage of losses. Even so, moral hazard can severely limit or even prevent the offering of insurance. Thus, while companies can readily offer you fire insurance for your home without too much concern that you will respond by leaving oily rags around the house and merrily tossing about lit matches, they may be quite unable to offer you attractively priced insurance against the quite substantial economic risk of having to sell your home for a loss. The problem here is that your actions in home upkeep and sales strategy or effort may be hard to monitor. The end result may be that you are forced to bear an undesired risk that is in principle diversifiable, due to the difficulty of credibly guaranteeing your good-faith effort to seek the best available price.

- Any other transaction costs of offering the insurance must not exceed what people are willing to pay for the coverage.

Where these problems prove sufficiently serious, private insurance will not be found. One therefore can speak of incomplete private insurance markets that fail to satisfy people's demand for protection from risk. Without more, however, this is merely cause for regret, like the fact that ice cream is fattening or that dinner dishes do not wash themselves. Both as individual consumers and as a society, we must do without things that are unavailable or that cost more than we are willing to pay for them.

What potentially creates a case for government intervention in mitigating people's risks—rather than just a variant of the old Monty Python question "What if Queen Victoria could fly?"—is some reason to think that the government can do better than private firms in addressing one or more of these obstacles to providing insurance. Indeed, for government intervention in completing insurance markets to be desirable, any such advantages must be great enough to make up for any special disadvantages that the use of government may bear due to defects in administrative efficiency or political incentive structures.

In some cases, the government may have superior information that facilitates addressing measurement problems or moral hazard (Auerbach and Kotlikoff 1995, 546). Or it may be able to provide cheaper coverage because everyone wants essentially the same thing and it can exploit economies of scale or save people the trouble of choosing a particular policy. However, the two remaining insurance problems provide the most far-reaching rationales for a government role in completing private insurance markets. Any government that controls a large enough territory for exit to be costly can address adverse selection, as private insurers cannot, by requiring people who are subject to its jurisdiction to enroll. And if political decisions are sufficiently stable, the government can try to commit people, such as the members of future generations, to particular risk-spreading arrangements that are impeded by the resolution of uncertainty before people are able to enter into explicit insurance contracts.

A final rationale for mandatory government insurance is controversial in practice, but plain in theory and undeniably influential in the Social Security setting. This is the paternalistic view that people should be protected from their own predictable errors, such as myopically failing to acquire coverage that they really should want (Diamond 1977, 281–83). Here (and also for adverse selection), if the government's advantage lies simply in its power to tell people to eat their spinach, then it need not go beyond requiring them to purchase a specified type of coverage from any suitable private firm.[1]

Risk-Spreading and Risk Prevention

The government's power to make people eat their spinach brings to mind another tool it can deploy in societal risk management. In general, risk-spreading is only one device for offering people protection against risks that various bad things will happen to them. The other big device is risk prevention, or reducing the likelihood that particular bad things will happen in the first place. An example is managing automobile accident risks, not just through conventional insurance that shares between the lucky and the unlucky the costs of such accidents as they occur, but also by requiring behavior that is likely to reduce accidents. Rules of this sort include barring children, along with adults under the influence of alcohol, from driving and imposing speed limits or seat belt requirements. The motivation for these rules may include both paternalism and concern about the costs you may impose on others through dangerous behavior.

In response to the moral hazard problem that arises if you will get money from the insurance company when you harm yourself, companies may offer incentives for cautious rather than reckless behavior, such as by raising your premium if you get a speeding ticket. However, they have less power than the government to induce risk-avoiding behavior that people do not choose on their own. As we will see, risk prevention is an important part of the Social Security picture, helping to show that social insurance need not be limited to the familiar risk-spreading tools of private insurance.

Social Insurance and Income Risk

The previous two sections suggested that the government's role in providing social insurance, in the sense of supplementing the risk mitigation accomplished by private markets, is potentially quite broad. Indeed, a social insurance rationale underlies not just Social Security but most of what the government does in the tax and transfer realms, and much regulatory policy as well. (Consider airline safety rules, food and drug policy, and securities regulation.) However, even among the tax and transfer rules most germane to Social Security reform, the term "social insurance" typically gets a much narrower interpretation, for reasons that may at one time have made political or expositional sense, but that should not prevent us from taking an appropriately broad view here.

The usual list of major "social insurance" programs in the contemporary United States is limited to Social Security, Medicare, unemployment insurance, and a few smaller related programs that address disability or retirement in specific industries (Steuerle et al. 1998, 83; Rosen 1995, 196). Consistently with how these programs operate, "social insurance" is typically defined to involve not just mandatory risk-sharing at the government's behest, but two features that seem to parallel private insurance arrangements. First, each participant ostensibly pays a distinct premium for the coverage, although the amount so paid need not determine the actuarial value of expected benefits. Second, benefit payments are not conditioned on any explicit income or other means-testing (Atkinson 1995, 205; Rosen 1995, 195).

This limited usage of the term "social insurance" has a historical cause. The programs with this label that emerged in the United States and England beginning with the Great Depression dispensed quite deliberately with means-testing. Proponents thought that limiting program benefits to the poor would both guarantee inadequate legislative funding and discourage participation by making it a humiliating confession of need (Atkinson 1987, 781). Having designed "universal" programs for people who experienced a given contingency such as losing their jobs or reaching retirement age, the proponents needed a novel term to signal that they were up to something new and different. The term "social insurance" seemed apt, since private insurance typically does not involve means-testing (Bill Gates can collect on his car insurance policy just like anyone else). Perhaps more importantly, the term helped give the programs an appealing and business-like air. People tend to like the idea of insurance coverage, so much so that "experimental studies have shown that . . . [they become] more likely to choose a sure loss over a larger probable loss if the former is called an insurance premium" (Shiller 1993, 19–20).

Be that as it may, when we consider the social insurance function—that is, the government's role in supplementing the risk mitigation accomplished by private markets—there is no reason to limit the inquiry to programs with a distinct premium and non-means-tested benefits. The first of these two attributes is insignificant. If participation is mandatory and what you pay does not much influence what you get, then it is pure Clown family accounting to think it even matters that some of your overall taxes are labeled "premiums" for the benefits. The government could do exactly the same things without purporting to charge separately for the coverage.

As for means-testing, there are three reasons why it does not contradict, and indeed in the big picture is indispensable to, the social insurance function. First, means-testing is inherently a kind of insurance, in that it addresses a particular risk: what one might call "income risk"—ignoring for this purpose (as I will throughout) whether "income," as opposed to, say, "consumption" or "wealth," is the specific measure of people's means that we ought to use.[2] Getting more compensation if your income is low than if it is high reduces the extent to which your overall well-being depends on your income level before the compensation was paid. Thus, insurance coverage should and must involve means-testing if income risk is among the things being insured against. To say that means-tested benefits are not insurance because they typically are absent from private insurance policies would be akin to saying that life insurance is not really insurance because it does not protect you against the risk of property damage from automobile collisions.

Second, the presence or absence of means-testing within a given program is not informative about the extent to which the government is addressing income risk. It is just a formal program attribute (or one with Clown family accounting significance) rather than one that is necessarily meaningful. Suppose that a demogrant, or uniform cash payment to all citizens or residents, were introduced, with the financing coming from an increase in income tax rates. This non-means-tested program would address income risk because the net effect of its introduction (given the financing mechanism) would depend on your pretax income level. The difference between an income tax–financed demogrant and a means-tested welfare system lies simply in whether the income-conditioned element lies inside or outside "the program" as officially defined.[3]

Finally, addressing income risk is absolutely fundamental to the social insurance concept. Indeed, if we treat the term "income" simply as a placeholder for the idea of an attempted comprehensive measure of people's overall relative material well-being and need, it is the fundamental thing that social insurance should be about. This is perhaps best explained, however, by dropping the term "income" as such and stating that social insurance, rather than focusing like most private insurance on particular risks such as car crashes or dying during your peak earning years while you have young dependents, should aim at risk writ large—at who ends up worst off versus best off overall, or at least with the greatest as opposed to the slightest needs that money can address.

Why should you want to insure against the risk that, say, your house will burn down or your car be stolen? The point is not just to hedge against the occurrence of a particular bad outcome. If it were that, dedicated sports fans would presumably bet heavily against their favorite teams, and religious parents might want to purchase insurance that would provide financial compensation if their children left the faith. The point of insurance, however, is not just to hedge but to provide money in states of the world where you will value it more rather than less, often due to the declining marginal utility of money but also given any other factors that affect need. (For example, if your long-standing chronic illness suddenly becomes treatable, you now have greater use for money than you previously did.)

The value of money in one state of the world compared to another depends on your overall circumstances. Among the relevant factors may be your current wealth and expected future earnings, what dependents you have who cannot provide for themselves, the force of any anticipated special financial needs such as for health care or education, and (through its effect on your physical condition) your age. On the latter point, Robert Shiller notes experimental evidence suggesting that the elderly are more risk-averse than the young, perhaps because severe financial loss is more dangerous given that their future earning prospects have faded and that they "will have much greater difficulty living as street people or beggars" (1998, 19).

The term "income risk" might need to be tortured somewhat to capture all the relevant circumstances, since "income" most naturally brings to mind a narrower set of financial transactions such as earning a wage. Even in this narrow sense, however, a focus on income risk pushes us far in the direction of looking at overall material circumstances. The insurance character of transferring money from high-income to low-income people is best recognized by the general public on the transfer side, where programs such as welfare and Food Stamps help provide what is commonly called the social safety net. Yet the income tax as well is essentially an insurance device so far as its distributional character is concerned. Whether you think of it as financing transfers to the poor (or for that matter to the members of powerful interest groups) or as paying for public goods such as national defense and police protection, its effect is to compress after-tax incomes relative to pretax incomes. Indeed, it has this effect so long as marginal tax rates are positive (so that the greater your income the more tax you pay), even if the rates stay flat or go down rather than being progressively graduated.

If income were simply a function of how hard you decided to work, it would not be risky and thus you would not need to insure it. In practice, however, people are subject to income risk of at least two kinds. One is that unpredictable circumstances beyond their control may determine their success or failure after they have acted, such as by starting a particular business or acquiring a particular workplace specialization. Businesses unpredictably succeed or fail all the time, and professions from oil production to legal work on corporate mergers and acquisitions are subject to surprise gains or losses from shocks to market demand or to competition from other suppliers. An income-based tax-transfer system mitigates these risks (Varian 1980).

The second form of income risk involves what one might call the ability lottery. People are born or somehow stumble into (be it from nature or nurture) varying abilities to convert effort into earnings. This could reflect their intelligence, looks, self-discipline, unscrupulousness, family connections, or whatever else makes some people economically more successful than others. So long as any uncertainty remains about your degree of good fortune in this regard, you are subject to a risk. Even once you know your "ability" level, however, it is natural to think: I was lucky or unlucky in how this lottery came out (as the case may be). And by extension: If I am risk-averse, I would have liked to insure against this risk had this been possible while I remained uncertain. Among public finance economists, at least since the famous (and recently Nobel Prize–rewarded) work of James Mirrlees (1971), the income tax has been conceptualized as an insurance mechanism to mitigate undesired risk from people's involuntary participation in the ability lottery.

This extension of insurance thinking may seem to push the envelope a bit. After all, the real-world income tax is implemented under the direction of voters who pretty well know how the ability lottery has come out for them. What is more, people who were sufficiently well-formed as individuals to make choices or even have preferences about insurance may inevitably have at least some inkling about the ability level that this notional lottery has dealt them. Yet, while these objections are pertinent to the question of how we should actually try, in an imperfect political world, to mitigate income risk through the tax-transfer system, at a basic conceptual level they can be disregarded. The idea of a "veil of ignorance," behind which you should make distributional judgments as if you did not know which of the people affected by them is actually you, helps to make the case for an insurance view. This idea is usually attributed to the philosopher John Rawls (1971) but really comes from the economist John Harsanyi, who justified it in terms of a morally required indifference between oneself and other people (1953, 435). To make a genuine value judgment about alternative income distributions rather than simply expressing crass self-interest, you must disregard how you in particular (compared to other people) would be affected by the outcome. This in turn requires "asking what sort of society [you] would prefer if [you] had an equal chance of being 'put in the place of' any particular member of the society," which is no less a risk problem than deciding on car insurance.[4]

In sum, therefore, income risk is well worth insuring against if you are risk-averse. Indeed, if the term "income," in any reasonably unstrained reading, did not fall so far short of capturing all the variables (such as age, health, or your children's need for schooling) that might affect the value of having more rather than less money in alternative circumstances, one might almost call income risk the only thing worth insuring against. Yet observing the inadequacy of the term "income" as a placeholder for all these factors only moves one further still in the direction of viewing insurance as having a single comprehensive aim: to shift the money that you might expect to have across all possible future states of the world from those where you think you would value it less to those where you think you would value it more.

A Single Comprehensive Insurance Measure?

My analysis of income risk suggests that the ideal insurance policy, considered without regard to such obstacles as adverse selection and moral hazard, would provide global coverage based on a single comprehensive, albeit multidimensioned, measure of need. It thus would not look like the private insurance we observe, which addresses discrete risks of fire, accident, and the like. Nor would it look much like the programs that are most commonly called social insurance, with their similar focus on discrete events such as getting sick or losing your job. Rather, the ideal insurance policy we might expect everyone to value would look more like an income tax integrated with transfers to the poor (perhaps using demogrants) and that adjusted as appropriate for various other discrete risks presently covered either through private insurance or through the existing government programs that everyone calls social insurance.

To be sure, one could get carried away in asserting that people really want a single comprehensive insurance offering. The claim is more normative than empirical; it describes what someone rationally seeking his own material self-interest from behind the veil ought to want, rather than what we see people demanding. Various arguments can be made for retaining at least some elements of isolated special-purpose insurance. For example, decision research reveals that people act inconsistently and dislike some losses more than others based on details of mental framing for different events (Kahneman and Tversky 1979). Just as a gambler might attach arbitrary significance to breaking even for the night as distinct from simply doing as well as possible, so people might want more insurance here and less there due to the psychic flavor that various losses would have for them, and without regard to the usefulness of a dollar under different circumstances. You might, for example, disvalue a $20,000 car accident loss either more or less than a one-time $20,000 drop in the value of your expected lifetime earnings.

Or consider the possible appeal of unemployment insurance. There are various reasons why I might decide behind the veil that if I lose my job, I will get temporary income support in excess of that which I would get simply by reason of being low income. Perhaps I would anticipate being habituated to affluence and needing time to adjust if things worsened for me permanently. Or I might imagine having various fixed expenses, such as under a home

mortgage, that would make it especially awkward to lose a comfortable income stream even if I anticipated getting it back. (This is a problem of
imperfect capital markets if I cannot borrow during temporary personal
downturns against earnings that I reasonably expect in the future.) Unemployment insurance might therefore be a special case where it makes sense to
transfer resources from the worse-off to the better-off, as it does compared
to straightforward progressive redistribution.

Perhaps, however, this example does more to show how complicated a
comprehensive ideal insurance scheme would be than to refute thinking in
broad terms. After all, the needs created by sudden job loss should presumably still be traded off against other needs. And it is in this sense of helping
us to think about sensible tradeoffs that the comprehensive insurance idea
really pays off. All too often, the political system addresses whatever needs
are on the front page or affect powerful interests, to the exclusion of perspective and balance. Thus, because we want to assure adequate medical
treatment to seniors in ill health, we spend hundreds of billions of dollars to
give them comprehensive Medicare coverage, even when they are quite
well-off, without any serious prioritizing of their needs and risks against
those of other people. Or we target federal disaster relief to the victims of
events that yield especially good television footage. Social insurance should
not be so haphazard and whimsical, even if we cannot all agree about its
ideal form.

Public versus Private Insurance Protection against Income Risk

What should we make of the fact that private insurance looks nothing like
the comprehensive package I have described? Again it tends to address only
discrete risks, such as car collision or fire, and to ignore income risk. Since
people show through their political preferences that they care about income
risk, the explanation, presumably, is that insurance companies find addressing it unfeasible despite hypothetical market demand.

One barrier to the offering of private protection against income risk
might be that the government is already in the business. Similarly, private insurers cannot make money by offering to compensate outright government
takings of property, since the government pays fair market value compensation without charging a premium. However, even if the government got out
of the income risk business, private insurers might be unable to go far beyond, say, offering fixed or inflation-indexed term or life annuity policies (the
private analogue to a demogrant, but with no transfer of expected value be-

tween subscribers). In particular, insurers cannot offer means-tested benefits, or even narrower unemployment coverage, unless they can adequately address concerns about (a) moral hazard, in the form of working less hard as your income grows more assured; (b) adverse selection, in the form of buying more insurance if you have inside information suggesting that your future income is likely to be low; and (c) the difficulty of offering insurance against some risks, such as that relating to income-earning ability, before they are resolved.[5]

Only if the government can do better than private firms in addressing income risk do we really have a case for it to intervene, rather than just another case of "wouldn't it be nice if Queen Victoria could fly." In general, the government has no unique ability to address moral hazard problems (except insofar as it can gather information more cheaply, as I discuss below). Indeed, moral hazard is the core reason why government protection against income risk must be limited. Effects on work incentives explain why neither total wealth equalization nor Marx's credo "From each according to his abilities, to each according to his needs" has worked in numerous historical trials (Shiller 1993, 1).

Adverse selection with respect to income risk is something that a government can address more effectively than a private insurer, so long as exiting its jurisdiction is costly. And perhaps a government can commit to the broad contours of a given policy before insured individuals are born (and thus start to learn how they have fared in the ability lottery), although this depends on the political stability of its decisions. Finally, its powers to compel information reporting and conduct audits, and perhaps to centralize administration if this brings scale efficiencies, may give it transaction cost advantages over a private firm in dealing with income risk.

The extra downside of using the government to address income risk must be kept in mind, however. Insurance that is justified partly with reference to what people would hypothetically agree to behind the veil (or if they weighed each others' interests equally with their own) may depart greatly from what the political system can provide. Political choices will inevitably reflect the interests of the actors given how things have turned out for them. The language of insurance can thus be misused in support of either extreme: leaving the unfortunate to starve, or engaging in confiscation at levels that unduly discourage work effort in the future. Or a political system that is free to redistribute as it chooses can simply be capricious, transferring wealth, say, to farmers or homeowners, or for that matter to Saddam Hussein, without any plausible insurance rationale. People's differing views about the gravity of these dangers relative to the benefits of well-executed social insurance naturally produce disagreement about the likely social gain or loss from government activity in mitigating income risk.

Is income risk all that the government should address? If we define income narrowly to refer only to earnings and the like, without regard to other factors that affect the value to someone of an extra dollar, then we plainly fall short of a suitably comprehensive measure. One could make a good case, however, for leaving out of social insurance the risks that people can sufficiently address through their private insurance choices. Examples might include home or car damage that is easy to insure against, medical expenses if the health insurance market is sufficiently well-functioning (Kaplow 1991), and the risk that a readily diversifiable investment such as tax-exempt municipal bonds will lose value due to a change in government rules (Shaviro 2000). Arguably, income risk narrowly defined is a very substantial part of what remains, thus helping to explain income's preeminent role on both the tax and transfer sides of distribution policy.

The Relevance of Household Status to Social Insurance

Even if income risk, narrowly defined, were the only proper subject of social insurance, we would still face some dilemmas in determining how best to mitigate it for a given individual. People are social creatures who take on partners and form family groups, rather than being uncompromising individualists like tomcats or green iguanas. We have already seen that the value you place on a dollar may be affected by the needs of any loved ones, but couples or families—households, in the more neutral language favored by economists—matter for additional reasons as well. If the members of a family or other household have any inclination to pool or share their resources, then the income enjoyed by one may affect the material circumstances experienced by others. The relevance of household, not just personal, income can readily be seen by asking: If Mrs. Bill Gates has zero income for the year, is she likely to have the same need for public assistance as a single mother with zero income? The answer is surely no, because we suspect that her spouse's material circumstances positively affect hers.

For this reason, tax and transfer systems in the United States and around the world take into account household circumstances of one kind or another. In particular, your marital status (sometimes extended to cover an unmarried cohabiting partner) and the number of dependents you are supporting may affect the tax you pay or the transfer you get. Thus, in the U.S. income tax, individuals who are married generally file joint returns under which the income of both spouses is included, and can claim personal exemptions for dependent children. Various welfare benefits also depend on the number of children and on a measure of household, not just individual, resources.

Given how household, not just personal, resources can affect personal circumstances, it is hard to see how any ambitious social insurance system could ignore information about the household.[6] Yet, even if household circumstances can be observed with sufficient accuracy, attempting to base outcomes on them may come at a considerable price in terms of moral hazard. For example, the American tax-transfer system is shot through with marriage penalties here and marriage bonuses there that create perhaps anomalous incentives to seek out or avoid the married state. If marriage affects—makes any difference in—how you are treated by a tax or transfer rule, then by definition it must be causing you to be treated either better or worse than if you were not married. And the same is true of genuine household status if that, rather than marital status, is observable and determines how you are treated.

The use of joint returns in the income tax helps illustrate a further moral hazard problem that can result from household taxation. Suppose that, in a "traditional" family where only the husband works, the wife is considering going to work. If the husband is a big enough earner, her first dollar of wages will be taxed at a high marginal rate, whereas in a purely individual system she could have earned a lot before high marginal rates kicked in. The result may be significant discouragement of entry into the labor market by women in traditional families, even if on balance such families receive a marriage bonus. Making the problem worse is the fact that women married to high-earning spouses, considered as a group, are highly tax-responsive (McCaffery 1997, 179–80), perhaps reflecting the influence of traditional gender roles along with the fact that if you engage in housework (such as raising your own children), you are a valuable but untaxed producer.

In sum, moral hazard reduces the extent to which it is desirable to base social insurance on marital or household status. People may respond to overall benefits or burdens of such status by changing their marital or household decisions in ways that are not independently desirable. And familiar moral hazard problems such as working less because your earnings are taxed may be exacerbated by the operation of marital or household taxation. Yet, in keeping with the significance of moral hazard generally, it does not necessarily follow that social insurance should be implemented wholly without regard to how your marital or household status affects your overall circumstances.

If Social Security Is the Answer, What Is the Question?

Let's return now to social insurance issues more generally, leaving aside Social Security's household aspects for the moment. If income risk narrowly defined were the sum total of what the government ought to insure against, one would face the question "Why Social Security?" A set of rules under which you pay tax during one period in your life and receive transfers during another might do no harm to a policy of mitigating income risk via progressive transfers, but would need some motivation to seem affirmatively worthwhile. If the elderly poor are not relevantly different than poor people in general, then Oscar Wilde's observation "It is better to have a permanent income than to be fascinating" (1948 ed., 219) suggests if anything universal demogrants, not retirement pensions, and a tax-transfer policy that takes no account of age should equally fit all. Obviously, however, the motivation for Social Security has something to do with considering age an important distributional factor, and therefore wanting to help the elderly, or at least the elderly poor.

Why might age matter? The apparently greater risk aversion of the elderly, reflecting that poverty is physically more dangerous for them (as well as more permanent if they can no longer work), is clearly relevant. Age might also arguably be relevant at levels well above basic subsistence if there were good evidence that it generally affects the usefulness of an extra dollar. Arguments that the elderly generally have greater use for wealth might note their greater expected medical needs (although these are insurable, as well as largely covered by Medicare) and that retirement brings extra leisure time, perhaps followed at some point by a need for greater assistance with daily chores. Arguments to the contrary might note that diminished physical capacity can affect the ability to consume in expensive ways (such as through ski trips to Switzerland).

A further reason why age might matter from a social insurance standpoint is that it could affect the costs of providing mandatory coverage—in particular, the significance of moral hazard in deciding whether to work. Older people who are considering retirement may be highly responsive to tax disincentives to work (Bankman and Griffith 1987, 1927), thus undermining the provision of coverage that is conditioned on their current work decisions. Once they are definitely retired, this issue may lie in the past for them, but moral hazard with regard to saving may remain a big problem if they can qualify for greater transfers by dissipating their wealth.

To examine how social insurance ought to respond to age differences, we can start by imagining that people did not observably age (in the sense of changing physically) over time, but instead had fixed physical characteristics throughout their lives. Thus, suppose each individual had throughout his or her life a set of attributes that we today associate with a specific age, and then died suddenly without any period of deterioration. That is, some would continually be more robust and others more frail until death came overnight.

Under these circumstances, we presumably would be especially keen to relieve poverty among the frail. Whether and to what extent we would make robust people, as opposed to nonpoor frail people, bear the costs of this extra income support would depend on our views concerning how members of the two groups differed in valuing an extra dollar once above the poverty level, and in posing moral hazard problems.

In such a world, would we provide frail people with fixed pensions (albeit not based on prior covered earnings, absent the life cycle) as we do with the old under actual Social Security? This, in effect, would be a demogrant for the frail, presumably paid for by income-related taxes on whoever was stuck with the bill. The answer is that it depends on all the usual considerations for choosing between income-conditioned benefits and demogrants; nothing is unique about it here. But in any event, those who were both frail and poor would receive a transfer from those who were more robust and/or wealthier.

In the real world, however, people pass through various life-cycle stages. They reach adulthood and then gradually become frail with age, presumably not to their complete surprise. (As the saying goes, they may be glad to age given the alternative.) This life-cycle phenomenon has two main implications for age-related social insurance. First, the need to have the government provide any insurance against age-related frailty is greatly reduced. Private insurers presumably can make good enough observations of prospective customers' age to mitigate age-based adverse selection.[7] And there is ample room for self-help by people as they age in an economy that provides many vehicles for saving and for choosing between alternative risk-return combinations. You can save when you are young if you want more income when you are old, and you can choose investment strategies that take account of your expected risk preferences at different stages in your lives.[8]

Second, providing income-conditioned aid to the elderly poor can generate special moral hazard problems that relate to life-cycle choices. If being both elderly and poor "pays off" better than being either one alone, you have an incentive to adjust your life-cycle choices in the direction of lesser accumulation, whether by working less or by spending more before retirement.

Why, then, have any age-related social insurance? The usual argument is one of paternalism, based on contrasting what people seemingly ought to do in their self-interest with what we observe they often do. The life-cycle model in economics (Modigliani and Brumberg 1954; Friedman 1957) holds that people, being rational, will take a farsighted view of how to allocate their consumption opportunities across their life spans, rather than following the shortsighted "eat when you kill" philosophy of the primordial savanna.[9] This generally implies—like the ant rather than the grasshopper in the fable— smoothing your consumption path relative to your earning path, since earnings may fluctuate but you will always need food, clothing, and shelter. Given the prospect of retirement, the life-cycle model strongly implies saving a significant fraction of income during your working years unless you expect to die young.

While advanced as an empirical prediction on the hypothesis that people act rationally, the model is most persuasive as an account of what type of consumption and saving behavior would be rational. Studies mainly suggest that people often violate life-cycle planning principles. For example, half of people in the middle-income deciles approach retirement with little accumulation, and retirement often prompts sharp belt-tightening, almost as if it had come as a surprise (Shiller 1998, 42). Perhaps the savanna was a poor training ground for a world with today's life expectancies and saving vehicles.

The apparently clear case for the optimality of life-cycle saving creates an inference, even for those (such as myself) who are often suspicious of paternalist arguments, that here is an instance where people would benefit from being forced to do something that we do not observe them doing on their own. Forced saving is therefore a kind of social insurance program, in the sense of responding to the risk of poverty when one is old that could have been avoided, and of a sort that private insurance obviously will not replicate. Strictly speaking, it is risk prevention, like imposing speed limits and requiring people to wear seat belts, rather than "true" insurance in the sense of risk-spreading. This difference in character means that it does not directly present moral hazard problems; you cannot game the system insofar as it forces you to do something whether you want to or not.[10] Instead, the main problems it poses are that on the one hand it might be ineffective (you negate the forced saving through your own separate dissaving), and on the other hand it might be excessive (you were right, from the standpoint of your self-interest and with no harm to anyone else, to want to save less).

Paternalism provides only one argument for forced saving, and perhaps not even the main one. A second argument is that if we are pained by seeing elderly people in poverty, we may want to ensure that they spare us this unpleasant sight by saving more earlier in their lives. In standard economics terminology, our discomfort at their poverty is a kind of externality, like pollution emitted by a factory, that those who would "inflict" it on us might be inclined to ignore. If the sight indeed pains us so much that we will pay to alleviate it and the prospective poor elderly can anticipate this, the problem turns back into moral hazard, which forced saving can help to eliminate. But calling it a sop to the queasy spectator, rather than to the person who is spared poverty in his old age, may appeal to the aesthetic taste for putting a rough coat over one's good nature that Adam Smith famously exemplified when he insisted that he gave alms to the poor out of selfishness, not charity, to ease his own discomfort at seeing their distress.

We now have a case for something that is starting to look like Social Security. All formalities aside, the system's most distinctive element is forced saving, as expressed by the timing of B versus T in my tautological Social Security equation (from chapter 3) under which $B = T + rT + X$ (that is, benefits equal taxes paid plus the investment return on them plus a positive or negative transfer). Other tax and transfer rules such as the income tax, welfare, and Food Stamps generally lack this feature (which is shared, however, with Medicare) since they do not mandate paying taxes first and receiving benefits later.

What about rT, the second term in the Social Security equation? This could, in principle, be kept as flexible as one liked. At the limit, one might require only that the funds actually be invested rather than spent, and give the taxpayer total freedom to pick the investment vehicle of his or her choice and bear the consequences of its performance for better or worse.[11] Social Security is currently at the other extreme, since it offers only an indexed life annuity. As we will see, while some proposed reforms to Social Security would expand (not just alter) investors' portfolio choices, nearly all would retain significant limits on choice. Not only will Albanian Ponzi schemes likely remain outside the permitted range, but few have proposed letting people bet their entire Social Security accounts on, say, a rise in short-term interest rates or a single hot Internet stock.

Limiting portfolio choice, like forced saving, is social insurance via risk prevention. The rationale, once again, is paternalism with a dollop of moral hazard. And the main downside, once again, is not moral hazard but rather the Scylla and Charybdis of ineffectiveness if Social Security participants can sufficiently adjust their overall portfolios to get wherever they like anyway, and excessiveness if they are prevented from making better choices in terms of their own preferences that would have harmed no one else.

What once again makes paternalism plausible is a fairly well-defined notion of optimality in investor choice. This notion has two main cornerstones: avoiding investments that lie below the risk-return frontier and minimizing overall risk through relatively safe choices and/or diversification. On the first of these points, it is often hard to say whether a given investment truly lies inside the risk-return frontier (although presumably those investing in it do not think so). All investments that turn on subsequent real-world outcomes, rather than simply being financial instruments with specified payoffs, may lack clearly observable odds up front. Even after the fact, you can only say how they turned out that time. Nonetheless, if we can identify a set of reasonably conventional investments that either offer decent specified payoffs or are popular and widely traded, we may be inclined to believe they lie, at the least, not too far below the "true" risk-return frontier that we might all agree about if we had better information. And we may want to insist on some degree of relatively fixed-return investment, or at least diversification, if we believe that investors who know what they are doing would choose these features in any event.

Obviously, it would be insanity to require in general that investment in our society follow safe or conventional paths. (The reader should feel free to insert here a few stock phrases about entrepreneurship and the vision of Bill Gates or Jeff Bezos or whichever New Age magnate is currently hot.) Still, as a residual matter and with an eye to the average investor, one could argue that some degree of forced restraint may reduce investor errors—along with "heads I win, tails you lose" bets on the transfer system—more than it takes away good opportunities. Indeed, if actual financial expertise tends to be positively correlated with the ability and inclination to undo for one's overall portfolio the effect of limiting investment choice for a part, then those who would be most likely to make bad choices may end up being the ones who are limited the most.

We have now very roughly rationalized a program that, like current Social Security, in some fashion has as key design elements T in advance of B and a constrained rT. What about X, or the use of Social Security to transfer wealth between participants? Here we are no longer in the realm of something that is fundamental or definitional to a system bearing the name. Not only are there myriad transfers outside of Social Security, but a Social Security system with no X element or a radically different set of transfers could still easily bear the name.

In many respects, it should be a matter of complete indifference whether any given transfer policy is executed inside or outside of Social Security. However, in a world where Clown family accounting often reigns, the use or nonuse of Social Security may make an important political difference. In addition, from a technical standpoint in achieving desired distributional results, the use of Social Security may have implications (whether favorable or adverse) for convenience and accuracy due to three of its key attributes: it pays attention to people's current ages, it pays attention to their years of birth, and it provides benefits based on information about career earnings rather than (like the income tax or Food Stamps) information that is largely limited to the current year. Here is why each of these factors might matter.

Social Security's Reliance on Age

Despite the moral hazard problems discussed earlier, forced saving may not fully do the job of age-adjusting the tax-transfer system, in particular by providing adequately for the elderly poor. Suppose someone is always too poor to support himself. He may be unable to save without great hardship and, under a system like the present one, may have accrued little in the way of covered earnings. Thus, forced saving may be of little help if we want to increase his public support when he is old. A system of retirement pensions called Social Security may conceivably be used to provide this aid, although the technical advantages of doing so, rather than directly making age a relevant factor in the welfare system, are unclear.

Social Security's Reliance on Year of Birth

Even when the physical consequences of aging are not themselves the subject of social insurance, people in different age cohorts might benefit from spreading risks that bear on them differently because of when they were born. Private markets generally cannot satisfy the demand for such coverage, however, despite the lack of moral hazard. (You cannot control your birth date or the broader social and economic trends that generate these risks.) The problem, rather, is that by the time people are in a position to make insurance agreements, the actual generational winners and losers are at least somewhat known. The government can therefore, at least in principle, remedy adverse selection by requiring everyone to enroll.

Perhaps the most obvious subject of such insurance is differences in average wealth between generations. The standard argument for progressive redistribution suggests that you would agree to transfers from wealthier to poorer generations if you did not know to which generation you would end up belonging. Although such transfers have nothing to do with forced saving or retirement pensions as such, Social Security provides a possible vehicle for making them, because at any time it is levying taxes on members of some generations and paying transfers to others (and possibly affecting future generations through benefit promises to current workers that may end up being hard to renounce).

A related problem is the ability of members of different age cohorts to reduce their risk exposure with respect to the short-term path of the economy by holding optimal diversified portfolios. During your working years, your own human capital is likely to be a huge component in your own portfolio, potentially leaving you and your fellow workers quite vulnerable to business downturns in the overall macroeconomy. (The risk of a downturn just in your sector presumably is handled by the income tax and safety net transfer programs.) By contrast, once you retire, your portfolio may reside in the financial markets, including the stock market. While the risks in the two sectors are clearly correlated, as in the case where a recession both wipes out jobs and sinks the Dow Jones average, they are not entirely in lockstep (Shiller 1998, 39). Thus, it is plausible that workers and retirees would like to achieve mutual increases in diversification by swapping human capital risk for financial capital risk. Yet transactions of this kind may be impeded by the difficulty of trading in your own human capital (Merton 1983, 327–28). Once again, Social Security provides a possible mechanism for these trades, if retirement benefits vary with the relative fortunes of workers and retirees.

Social Security's Access to Information about Career Earnings

Social Security applies a kind of lifetime perspective to progressivity insofar as benefits depend on earnings throughout your career. To be sure, in its present form it is sensitive to arbitrary details of your annual wage path, given the annual ceiling on covered earnings and the use of dropout years. Still, it is far closer to a lifetime measure than the almost completely annualized income tax (Diamond 1977, 278) and safety net transfer programs.

This long-term focus potentially makes Social Security a convenient tool for increasing the extent to which overall distribution policy focuses on people's lifetime earnings, rather than, like an annual tax with graduated marginal rates, transferring wealth between those with bouncy versus smooth earnings paths. To be sure, the fact that Social Security only provides retirement pensions is a disadvantage with respect to this function. Your lifetime earnings increasingly become known as your career proceeds, yet the system does not begin paying you until you have retired. This presumably reduces the value of the lifetime redistribution to its beneficiaries unless they can effectively borrow in advance against the value of their expected benefits. Any such reduction serves no good end to the extent that lifetime redistribution is the aim without regard to forced saving.

Issues Posed by Households in a Social Security–Type System

So far, my discussion of what social insurance purposes a Social Security–type system might serve has ignored questions of household structure. However, it is fairly easy to see a few main implications. One is that a household with two retired individuals needs greater financial resources to escape dire poverty than a household with just one retired individual. This suggests requiring greater forced saving by married couples than by single individuals with the same lifetime income—the point being not that married couples should necessarily save a greater percentage of their earnings (their needs may be greater throughout adulthood), but rather that the floor on what is a rational amount to save for retirement may be higher.

The difference in need has implications for transfer policy as well as forced saving. Again, there is a strong social insurance argument, subject to the usual moral hazard considerations, for transfers from smaller to larger households that have the same overall resources.[12] These need not be retirement transfers if sufficient forced saving is being required, but they can be. And in comparing household size at retirement, the main difference lies between those with one versus two members—single versus married if we ignore the important fact that not all true couples are married. Retirees' children have mainly ceased to be dependents and may indeed be capable of aiding their parents. Thus, if they were taken into account at all, the most frequent implication might be to reduce the measured need to provide retirement support to parents.

A Social Security–type system that applies on a purely individual basis will tend to increase forced saving and retirement benefits for married as compared to single households with comparable primary earners if, but only if, both of the spouses work. In addition, the only transfer content of such a system as between the two types of households will be whatever results from applying more general redistributive policies, such as from high earners to low earners and from people with short life expectancies to people with long life expectancies. Perhaps this would be fine, given the opportunities for redistribution between households in, say, the income tax and welfare systems, if not for one important fact about many households: that married women, especially if they have children, often participate far less in the labor market during their working years than do other adults. Women (or men) who stay home may to some extent benefit through the tax-transfer system from doing so—for example, because the value of the household services they provide, unlike the market work they might have chosen instead, is not taxed. But a Social Security–type system that applies on a purely individual basis may fail to provide these individuals with the retirement resources they need, especially though not exclusively after their spouses die, unless it comprehensively takes adequate care of people with extremely low career earnings.

To put the problem more generally, a Social Security–type system in a society with traditional one-earner married households faces a "retired houseworker problem" that can be handled through one or more of the following departures from a pure individual model in which only workers get retirement benefits:

- *The pure forced saving route:* increase wage taxes on traditional households in order to increase their retirement benefits without transfer consequences;
- *The forced saving of a transfer route:* just increase retirement benefits for such households, so that at retirement they get a transfer from other households; or
- *The broader demogrant route:* provide adequately for nonworkers in general, presumably through transfers paid after retirement whether or not household status is taken into account.

How Well Does the Design of Social Security Fit Its Social Insurance Function?

How well does the actual Social Security system perform the social insurance functions that one could contemplate assigning to a system bearing the name? Let's look in turn at the main such functions that I suggested in the previous section.

Forced Saving

By definition, a system that uses wage taxes to fund retirement pensions results in forced saving by its participants within its formal boundaries. If there is forced saving overall, then, depending on your view about its proper level, the current system might be requiring either too little of it or too much. An aim of increasing forced saving would suggest raising tax and benefit levels on a distributionally neutral basis, while an aim of reducing it would suggest lowering them.

Either way, however, Social Security clearly results in forced saving unless people offset their Social Security wealth by running up such a high level of net personal debt that their benefits are in effect forwarded to the lenders as debt service. This does not generally appear to be happening (Mulligan and Sala-i-Martin 1999b, 19). Many households may accumulate little in the way of positive financial assets by retirement (Feldstein 1998, 11), but they are considerably more likely to hold home equity wealth than to be in the minus column, Social Security aside.

The fact that people generally do not dissave their Social Security wealth in advance does not, of course, prove that it actually increases anyone's saving. If, in its absence, each participant would have saved enough more to make up for the lack of Social Security wealth (ignoring the system's transfer content), then it is merely forcing a nation of Popeyes to eat their spinach. However, most observers agree that some people would reach retirement with less than the Social Security wealth we observe if the system's forced saving element were eliminated.[13]

Martin Feldstein, the most prominent advocate of the view that Social Security significantly reduces aggregate national saving, calculates that "existing Social Security wealth reduces overall private saving by nearly 60 percent" (1998, 12). Yet even a 100 percent figure would indicate only that the forced saving strategy was unnecessary, not that it was failing, to the extent that people were merely substituting Social Security wealth for private wealth accumulation, rather than using it to run up private disaccumulation. And Feldstein's claim that Social Security reduces national saving, while important (and to be discussed in chapter 5), mainly concerns macroeconomic policy, not social insurance, since it turns on an argument about overall welfare rather than risk distribution. As I noted in chapter 3, if someone promises to pay you money in the future, you have a form of saving, although national saving is not directly affected since the promise is equivalently dissaving by the promisor.

Portfolio Choice

Social Security clearly and sharply limits portfolio choice within its boundaries by offering only one benefit package to each participant. Suppose you wanted to do any of the following: (a) increase your risk and expected return by causing your benefit level to depend on the performance of the stock market, (b) eliminate political risk by swapping your expected benefits for legally enforceable government debt, or (c) eliminate your life expectancy bet within Social Security by selecting a benefit, such as a fixed-term annuity, that had the same payout no matter what your life span and was even inheritable. None of these choices is permitted to participants within Social Security.

Once again, the limitations might be ineffective due to the outside adjustments that people make. For example, the extent to which many relatively well-heeled but risk-averse investors hold corporate stock rather than indexed bonds or fixed real annuities in their private portfolios may reflect that Social Security helps to satisfy their taste for having a fixed real-return asset in their portfolios. Permitting such investors to participate in the stock market through Social Security might have no effect on their overall portfolios.

From a social insurance standpoint, however, the reason for limiting choice is presumably just to require that some minimum portion of the investor's portfolio consist of a fixed real annuity, rather than in general to tilt overall portfolios in some direction. It seems clear that this aim is generally met, at least as to most of the people with a significant risk of being poor upon retirement. Households that lack positive financial assets at retirement generally just have what Social Security gives them, along with any home equity. And I am unaware of any evidence, even anecdotal, that those with home equity respond to Social Security by making risky debt-leveraged bets in the real estate market via their homes.

In addition, consider participation in the stock market, which is evidence of wanting at least some risk given the payoff in expected return, and which also (coupled with the use of debt) might be a key element in trying to negate the system's impact on one's overall portfolio. As of 1995, 59 percent of the U.S. population did not hold stocks, even through mutual funds or private pension plans (Geanakoplos, Mitchell, and Zeldes 1998, 29). While in theory these people might be so averse to the stock market that if forced to participate in it through Social Security, they would simply "short" out this participation by placing matching side bets that pay off as stock prices decline, few believe that this is the case, or that very many of these people have the financial resources or savvy to do so conveniently.[14]

Social Security therefore apparently does succeed in affecting at least some people's overall portfolio positions. While this suggests that its limiting portfolio choice does indeed have social insurance significance, there is ample room to debate the desirability of the particular limits that it imposes. This question is usually posed in terms of stock market participation. The system could be changed to permit or require people to place some or all of their Social Security wealth in the stock market and then bear the actual outcomes, as under a typical "privatized" system with individual investment accounts. Or, without any expansion of investor choice through Social Security, the government could buy stocks (perhaps through the Social Security Trust Fund) and generally adjust benefit payments in accordance with how the stock performed.

Either way, the change presumably would reflect viewing the current level of risk mitigation as excessive. A second motivation might be the view that people are irrationally averse to stock market risk, and thus on paternalist grounds ought to have their toes dipped in the water whether they like it or not (Smetters 1999, 210).

Other changes to the existing choice parameters are possible as well. Thus, suppose we permitted people to opt for smaller annual payments in exchange for some potential to bequeath unpaid benefits to their heirs if they died relatively young, or to bet on low inflation by selecting a nonindexed benefit package. Or people might be permitted to eliminate Social Security's downside political risk by choosing in advance to receive smaller payments that had the legal status of enforceable debt.

Progressive Redistribution Based on Career Earnings

The mitigation of lifetime income risk that Social Security accomplishes by combining a flat rate tax on covered earnings with a declining-rate benefit formula is, at least by some measures, quite substantial—notwithstanding the somewhat offsetting effect of causing lifetime benefits to depend on life expectancy, which generally is greater in high-earning households. According to Caldwell et al., the current Social Security system is on a path to reduce lifetime income variance by 6 to 9 percent for age cohorts born between 1945 and 1959, and 10 to 13 percent for age cohorts born between 1960 and 2000 (1999, 35). These estimates ignore federal and state income taxation of Social Security benefits, which would tend to make the measured progressivity still greater (2).

The bad news about this insurance coverage is that the "premium" paid by post–World War II age cohorts is so high that winning simply takes the form of losing less than your higher-earning peers. Lifetime net tax rates under Social Security (in my terminology, X divided by lifetime income) are positive for all income deciles in all post–World War II age cohorts. Thus, even the poorest 10 percent of the people born in any year since World War II lose from the system, apart from any benefit to forced saving and limiting portfolio choice. What Social Security's progressive redistribution therefore means for these age cohorts is simply that the collective burden of paying for the transfer to older cohorts has been distributed progressively. Even at the bottom of the distribution, average lifetime income would be higher if not for Social Security.

From the standpoint of post–World War II generations, one might be inclined to say: A nuclear attack would have been better insurance still, since dropping everyone to zero would completely eliminate income variance. Obviously, for insurance to be attractive, there must be cases where it leaves you better off. Still, even apart from the insurance argument for a transfer to pre–World War II age cohorts (which I discuss next), once it is effectively irrevocable, the cost of paying for it becomes a real burden that younger generations must distribute, along with all other benefits and burdens of the world in which they find themselves, in one way or another. There is no reason to denigrate Social Security's effect on income risk simply because one may be inclined to associate it with the generational transfer that happens to have been implemented through the same set of rules.

How, then, should we view Social Security's insurance effect with regard to income risk within an age cohort? In part, this depends on how you view progressive redistribution generally. Mitigating income risk is an important though controversial goal, at least implicitly accepted (despite any protestations to the contrary) by anyone who prefers a work-based tax, such as the current income tax or a consumption tax, to a uniform head tax under which everyone would owe the same amount. But estimates of both its gross benefit and its efficiency cost, at any given level of provision, vary enormously across the political spectrum. All we can really say here is that Social Security's distributional impact is an important element in any proposed reform, all too easily obscured if we direct our attention simply to restoring the system's long-term fiscal balance.

In a rational political world, the question of how much to redistribute could be substantially unlinked from the question of what role Social Security should play in the redistribution. As we have seen, the system's technical suitability as a supplement to the annually based income tax and safety net transfer systems depends on the tradeoff between the virtue of its access to information about career earnings and the vice (to the extent forced saving is not the goal here) of its not paying off before retirement. Real-world political choices may be more constrained, however, at least in the short run. Simply because politicians and voters make artificial distinctions between formally separate fiscal systems without sufficiently grasping that the whole is what matters, your preference regarding redistribution through post-reform Social Security might very well turn on how much redistribution you favor, rather than on the attributes of this particular tool.

In any event, however, Social Security's performance in measuring people's lifetime earnings for redistributive purposes could probably be improved. As discussed in chapter 2, such features as its ignoring annual earnings above the ceiling, ignoring earnings in dropout years, and rewarding single-earner couples guarantee that its distributional impact will often be quite odd. And the fact that its tax and benefit formulas operate separately, each receiving frequent ad hoc adjustment, can impede executing a coherent distribution policy.

Redistribution Based on Age or Year of Birth

The convenience of using Social Security to transfer wealth between people in different life-cycle stages and age cohorts has been exploited frequently, beginning in the 1930s with the windfall to the first generation of covered retirees and continuing thereafter with tax and benefit changes from which current retirees almost never lose. In directing overall poverty prevention efforts toward the elderly through transfers above and beyond forced saving, Social Security has if anything been too effective, given the competing claims of other age groups, such as the very young, that cannot muster the same political power (Shaviro 1997a, 142). But in aiding earlier-born at the expense of later-born age cohorts, Social Security plainly has pointed in the right direction with respect to mitigating income risk. As Dean Baker and Mark Weisbrot rhetorically ask: "How many Generation X-ers would trade their grandparents' return on Social Security taxes and also their lifetime income for their own? So far we have not found anyone who would like to make that trade" (1999, 35).

This success of Social Security from a social insurance standpoint, accomplished through periodic ad hoc tax and benefit adjustments, strongly depends upon the fact that so long as society keeps getting wealthier, the age group (elderly people) with the greatest political power is also generally the poorest on a lifetime basis. The current system might look less appealing if we asked: How would it respond to different contingencies, such as an economic downturn that left young people worse off than the elderly? This could happen, for example, if a recession hit the labor market harder than the stock market.

Under such circumstances, transfers from the elderly to the young, or at least reduced transfers in the other direction, might be appropriate. But the adoption of such transfers through Social Security would be impeded not only by the power of the AARP, but also by an ideology that holds that benefits currently promised to the elderly can be increased but not reduced. This one-way ratchet results in risk-transferring between age cohorts with respect to the impact of a recessionary shock, as opposed to risk-spreading or overall risk mitigation. This is not insurance at all from an aggregate social standpoint.

Treatment of Households

By providing spousal benefits to individuals who may have concentrated on housework while their spouses did most of the earning, Social Security responds to the greater post-retirement needs of a two-person compared to a one-person household in the setting where the system's otherwise individual structure would not otherwise have this effect automatically. Plainly, there is a good social insurance rationale for responding in some way to the retired houseworker problem. However, there is much to criticize about exactly how Social Security responds, in particular:

- *Pure forced saving versus forced saving of a transfer:* A worker does not pay extra taxes for the spousal benefits that may end up going to his household. Thus, if the stay-at-home spouse never earns a wage that is subject to Social Security tax, the benefits are a pure transfer relative to the case of paying the same taxes but not getting spousal benefits. The more the secondary-earning spouse works, and thus pays Social Security taxes without increasing the household's benefits, the smaller the transfer to this household by reason of the spousal benefit. At some point, the transfer is eliminated altogether as the secondary earner switches over to claiming self-earned benefits.

  As I noted earlier in this chapter, the case for providing greater retirement benefits to a household with greater retirement needs is not identical to the case for making greater lifetime transfers to that household. The former may to some extent just be a case for increasing forced saving by that household of its own earnings. The existing scheme would therefore be subject to challenge on distributional grounds even if we were to stipulate that it gave everyone the right minimum level of retirement income.

  As it happens, the current system's distributional scheme between households has been attacked on all sides in the Social Security debate. The question of exactly how, all things considered, the tax-transfer system should bear on different types of households—taking account not just of Social Security but of all other relevant rules (such as those in the income tax)—goes well beyond the scope of this book. But the Social Security scheme of so substantially benefiting one-earner married couples at the expense of two-earner couples and single individuals is hard to defend. When you consider as well the basic effect of the income tax, which is to give marriage bonuses to one-earner couples while imposing marriage penalties on two-earner couples (Gravelle 1998, CRS-23), the level of overall benefit to one-earner households seems more dubious still.

- *Size of the spousal benefit for different households:* Also quite dubious on distributional grounds is Social Security's method of basing the spousal benefit on the earnings of the primary earner. Under this method, the spouse of a high earner gets more than the spouse of a low earner, despite the fact that the spouse of the low earner seems likely, all else equal, to have greater rather than lesser needs. From a social insurance standpoint, it seems precisely backward to have the benefit vary inversely to need (Steuerle and Bakija 1994, 208). Many other countries with social security systems that address the retired houseworker problem avoid this backward structure by providing either a flat spousal benefit or a minimum retirement benefit for all nonworkers (210).

- *Incentive effects of the spousal benefit:* A final problem with the spousal benefit goes to its incentive effects. Given that secondary earners, such as the wife in a traditional household, are highly tax-responsive, the fact that Social Security often bears on them, at the margin, as a pure tax may drive or keep a lot of them out of the workforce. Tradeoffs between social insurance and moral hazard are familiar, but here it is plausible that the price is too high, or at least could be greatly lowered relative to the social insurance benefits that are being achieved.[15]

I will leave for chapters 6 through 8 the question of how one might try to improve Social Security's treatment of household issues (and more generally that of reaching retirement age without having done much market work). For now, it is enough to note that even many supporters of the current system find its performance in this area to be inadequate and therefore in need of restructuring.

Summary

Insurance is a mechanism for responding to risk by directing your claims on resources to states of the world where they are worth more to you rather than less. "Social insurance" is a buzzword for government programs that respond to market failure in addressing undesired risks. Its main advantage lies in cases where the government is better situated than a private company to handle impediments to the cost-effective provision of insurance. For "true" insurance in the sense of risk-spreading, the government's most likely source of competitive advantage is its ability to address adverse selection by requiring some category of individuals within its jurisdiction (such as everyone) to participate. However, social insurance can also usefully be defined to include risk mitigation, such as imposing speed limits and seat belt requirements, and here once again the government's power to issue commands can, if rightly directed, make it the best available instrument.

The term "income risk," pertaining above all to the set of opportunities that nature, nurture, or sheer good fortune (along with your own choices and efforts) end up placing in front of you, can be used to describe the main area where social insurance can play an important role. Income risk has an age-related element since poverty tends to be worse if you are physically more feeble, as age tends to make us all. People can to some extent address the age component of income risk through their own life-cycle choices, such as saving adequately during their working years, but there is considerable evidence that they are prone to various kinds of predictable error.

A principal response of any social insurance system that we would recognize as Social Security is to impose risk mitigation through forced saving and limited portfolio choice. The aim here is simply to rule out certain choices, rather than to steer people's life-cycle and investment choices in general. Thus, reducing your outside saving in response to the forced saving through Social Security does not defeat the underlying social insurance policy unless you reach the point of net dissaving outside the system. This does not appear generally to be happening, although the fact that the policy therefore "succeeds" on its own terms tells us nothing about its relationship to the optimum.

The existing Social Security system also engages in considerable redistribution, an area of greater overlap with other tax-transfer programs such as the income tax and welfare systems. Here, Social Security appears on balance to transfer resources in the right direction (from richer to poorer people) due to its effects both within a given age cohort under constant tax and benefit rules, and between age cohorts given how these rules have changed over time. In some ways the transfers may be poorly directed, however. For example, the transfers resulting from its spousal benefit may make little sense even accepting that the number of retirees in a household is relevant to need and that some provision must be made for the support of retired houseworkers.

The analysis in this chapter is unlikely to suggest universally accepted answers to the question of how, if at all, the Social Security system should change. But it does, I hope, help to pose the issues properly. For too long, the

Social Security debate has been dominated by gibberish about saving the Social Security system (as distinct from helping the people whom it affects) or about "investing" the budget surplus in the Trust Fund and/or the Trust Fund in the stock market, without an adequate focus on what these policies would actually do. Perhaps political rhetoric can do no better. But thoughtful people should be focusing directly on the questions of what forced saving policy we should have, what portfolio choices should be offered with respect to forced saving, and what transfer policy we should follow, both inside and outside the Social Security system.

5 The Social Security Trust Fund: The Economics of Funding and the Politics of Accounting

Despite the importance and controversiality of the many policy issues that Social Security raises, its prominence in current political debate is almost entirely the product of a much narrower problem: the projected long-term inadequacy of its taxes to pay for its benefits. This financing problem, by putting Social Security reform on the agenda, provides a vehicle for raising other issues, such as concern about current generations' relatively bad deal from the system and interest in exploiting a prolonged stock market run-up. Without the financing problem, however, only proposals to sweeten the pot with no admitted downside for any current voter (at least through Social Security itself) would receive significant attention.

Social Security's long-term financing problem has both a purely formal element, in the sense of being an artifact of legal rules and accounting conventions, and a related underlying economic element. The formal element pertains to the Social Security Trust Fund, which is a legally mandated "series of bookkeeping entries" (Committee on Ways and Means 1996, 71) maintained by the Treasury Department to keep track of the revenues and outlays that are officially credited to the Social Security system. As a matter of law, the Treasury Department cannot pay Social Security benefits in excess of the Trust Fund balance (59). Exhaustion of the Trust Fund would thus serve as a trigger mechanism requiring express congressional action to keep benefits flowing. The 1999 Annual Report of the Social Security Board of Trustees projects Trust Fund exhaustion to occur in 2036,[1] although the recent trend has been for new forecasts to move this date back slightly. Far off though 2036 may now seem, it should be of considerable interest to most people who are alive today: it is the year when someone born in 1969 would reach the by-then normal Social Security retirement age of 67; and most people born after World War II have some hope of still being alive in 2036.

I call this aspect of the financing problem purely formal (which is not to say unimportant) because it depends on changeable legal rules that give force to certain accounting conventions. Suppose that Congress next year enacts legislation declaring that the Treasury's spending authority in Social Security is not limited to the Trust Fund, or that the Trust Fund will henceforth be credited with $2 for every $1 of Social Security taxes paid into it, or that $10 trillion should be added to the Trust Fund balance. The formal financing problem, involving the possible activation of the trigger mechanism, would vanish with the stroke of the president's pen upon signing this legislation.

There is, however, a related economic phenomenon to which the formal financing problem bears some relationship. Social Security taxes actually are projected to fall increasingly short of Social Security benefits with the passage of time, reaching annual deficit (according to the 1999 Report) in 2015 and by 2073 covering only about two-thirds of annual benefits. This may pose a problem either because we insist that, under some plausible computation, Social Security taxes actually equal (and thus can be said to pay for) Social Security benefits over time, or because of an overall shortfall of government revenues relative to outlays that causes political or economic difficulty.

As we will see, a lot of the Social Security financing debate is not about this economic phenomenon at all—it is purely about Trust Fund accounting conventions. As silly as this debate can sometimes be, arbitrary choices of accounting convention may actually matter simply because people act as if they do. Think of the Cowardly Lion, who actually became brave once the Wizard of Oz gave him a medal for valor. Nonetheless, I start with the economics to help situate what is really at stake in the debate over Social Security financing. The relevant issues go beyond the social insurance questions that I have emphasized so far, to reach concerns about the level of national saving, about trying to precommit our political system to making good decisions in the future, and about what sort of influence the government should have over resource allocation in the private sector.

The Relevance of Funding for Private versus Public Retirement Plans

The Social Security Trust Fund is not just any old trigger mechanism. Rather, it is one based specifically on the idea of enforcing a particular long-term relationship between Social Security taxes and benefits. In some respects, it can be compared to a printout that states your bank account balance (and thus limits the amount you can withdraw) without actually holding funds (Committee on Ways and Means 1996, 71). The self-financing aim serves political precommitment purposes that I discuss later in this chapter, but for now I just note that it makes Social Security look somewhat like a privately operated retirement system, such as a pension plan run by a company for its employees.

The analogy between a private retirement plan and public ones such as Social Security has been so influential that it requires discussion. To some extent, it is an identity, not just an analogy: a retirement plan is a retirement plan. However, a government plan has several distinctive features that we should always keep in mind, in particular:

- Private retirement plans are subject to greater risk of default from bankruptcy. A worker will naturally ask: Will the funds to pay my pension actually be there when I retire? By contrast, a national government that can print currency and extract revenues from a large-scale economy faces little risk of being unable to pay obligations that it accepts.

- Private retirement plans often involve enforceable contracts negotiated at arm's length. My employer might have a selfish interest in defaulting down the road if not constrained by reputational considerations (or, for that matter, business ethics). However, it can credibly precommit against doing so (subject only to bankruptcy risk) by offering a legally binding contract. The news for participants in a government plan such as Social Security is both better and worse. It is better insofar as you can, in effect, engage in self-dealing to the extent you hold political power. The government will not want to renege on paying you if you control it. On the other hand, your situation is worse from the irrevocable precommitment standpoint insofar as the government cannot, or at least does not, accept a contractual obligation even to the extent of issuing enforceable debt instruments to participants.

- As discussed in chapter 4 regarding adverse selection, the government can mandate participation within its jurisdiction, and thus deliberately transfer wealth between participants. Your country may be harder to leave than your job. Accompanying this greater power may be a set of policy aims that one might not expect to see in the private setting. In addition to any redistributive aims, the government may want to affect macroeconomic aggregates such as the level of work or saving in the society.

These differences often are underappreciated in comparing the financing of Social Security to that of a private retirement plan. In the private setting, the question of to what extent the plan's obligations are currently funded acquires an importance that does not fully translate to the public setting. Indeed, current funding is essentially *the* financing question posed by private plans, for reasons that do not entirely carry over to public plans.

Suppose you are considering working for a company that offers a retirement plan as part of its compensation package. The employer tells you that, under some formula, you will earn deferred income that is payable when you retire. A natural question to ask—as many employees learned the hard way under the first big wave of employee retirement plans early in the twentieth century—is how you can be sure of being paid. A contractual obligation to pay you is very nice, but it would be better still if the company showed you the money, and indeed irrevocably set it beyond the reach of the owners' caprice and rival creditors. So a separate bank account out of which retirement pensions will be paid, having the legal character of a trust fund that is reserved exclusively for this purpose, may be important to your peace of mind. You may also insist on grounds for confidence that the bank account will be big enough to pay your benefits when the day comes.

Thus, the extent to which a retirement plan is funded, in the sense of having assets set aside that will grow sufficiently to pay benefits, is often central in the private setting. For a government plan, you might have greater hope of being paid without funding, and by the same token you might have lesser hope of being paid with funding. The government will never be unable to pay like a bankrupt debtor, it may be eager to pay you even if it could renege, and if it does not want to pay you then a set-aside may not help (apart from possibly creating a sense of political precommitment). Funding thus does not matter in the same way or to the same extent as under a private plan.

What saves the degree of funding of a federal retirement plan from complete irrelevance, attempted political precommitment aside, is the fact that the government may have distributional and macroeconomic aims that it pursues through the plan. Suppose for the moment (perhaps unrealistically) that taxes and government spending outside the plan are unaffected by the extent to which it is funded. Then the degree of funding may matter in a couple of broad respects. Distributionally, funding means that the plan is paid for (presumably through tax contributions) as benefits accrue, rather than later as in an underfunded plan, or sooner as in an overfunded plan. Changing the time when taxes are levied may change the identity of who pays, most obviously between generations. From a macroeconomic standpoint, the degree of funding may affect the level of national saving—although the question of how it affects saving is quite complicated.

The main reason funding potentially affects saving is that it is indeed a form of saving *within the plan*. In a funded, compared to an unfunded, plan, assets have been set aside to provide a return for the future. And while money or financial instruments, perhaps the most likely assets for a retirement plan to hold, are not real assets (a country generally does not make itself wealthier by printing more currency), using them to save presumably means that more real investments are being made somewhere. Thus, in a federal retirement plan, more current taxes means more current funding means greater forced saving by current participants, who cannot spend the taxes they have paid on current consumption unless they borrow on the side against the value of expected future benefits.

Why isn't the degree of funding a perfect measure of a plan's effect on saving? Three factors make what is going on inside the system potentially misleading as to the overall effect. First, participants may respond to their forced saving through the plan by saving less outside the plan. Second, the fact that the government has extra assets on hand may affect its other tax and spending decisions. Third, the existence of transfers within the plan gives rise to income effects. People may adjust their saving (along with other choices) due to gaining or losing lifetime wealth via the transfers.

To illustrate possible income effects, suppose the government hands you a bond that you can redeem when you retire in thirty years for $100 million. The stated financing device is a uniform head tax of just a few dollars per person on all living individuals who are 25 years old on the redemption date. Thus, the bond's financing is fully specified, although it is unfunded because nothing is being set aside today. It seems plausible that you will respond to this bonanza by immediately starting to run up your current consumption spending. Why save your own current resources when you have this retirement bond to count on? More generally, transferring wealth from people who are high marginal savers to those who are low marginal savers generally reduces national saving, and people as yet unborn are a pretty clear case of current zero savers (ignoring possible responses today by their parents or grandparents).[2]

Greater current funding may tend to increase national saving insofar as it means that people alive today, who can save, are paying for benefits in lieu of unborn people who cannot yet save. Nonetheless, there is no simple equivalence between the degree of funding and the plan's income effect on saving. Different people who are alive today may have different marginal propensities to save, and thus the distribution of winners versus losers among the living will also have important income effects.

Why should the government care about the level of national saving? Here the social insurance argument from chapter 4, that people ought in their best interest to save at least some minimum amount for retirement, is not germane. Even if some people undersave during their working years, others may oversave. Examples might include young people with low current income but great future earnings prospects (economically a type of saving in human capital) against which they cannot borrow, and perhaps middle-aged neurotics who in their fright accumulate a larger nest egg than they really need. In the Great Depression of the 1930s, when oversaving writ large may have helped perpetuate the economic collapse (by shrinking current demand for consumption goods without any indication of when demand would recover), John Maynard Keynes argued that people might save simply "to satisfy pure miserliness, i.e. unreasonable but insistent inhibitions against acts of expenditure as such" (1964 ed., 108).

Claims that people are irrationally saving too little provide only one part of the argument that national saving is too low. Many note as well that the income tax penalizes saving (Seidman 1999, 32). In addition, one can deploy the classic externality argument from economics, which holds that my behavior may not be for the best if I have no incentive to consider its effect on other people. Saving leads to capital accumulation that may increase the material well-being of people as yet unborn (and who thus cannot affect our current saving decisions), although how much we should care about this if they will be wealthier than us in any event is debatable (Shaviro 1997a, 181–82).

While positive externalities suggest there may be too little saving, a claim of negative externalities can be made as well. In the Keynesian view of the Great Depression and recessions generally, savers signal personal pessimism about the future that may trigger a herd response by people who observe their caution, potentially leading to a sharp cyclical downturn in the economy until nearly everyone is worse off. A few people still suggest that the United States faces this problem today (Eisner 1998, 35).

Today's universal mantra, of course, is that the level of national saving is too low, rather than too high. However, this consensus brings to mind Mortimer Adler's six proofs of the existence of God. Proof One, he once told a University of Chicago audience, was that people in all societies have believed in Him. Proof Two—but here a voice from the audience broke in. "If the first proof was so good," someone asked Adler, "why do you need the other five?"

Still, while the sentiment for increasing national saving is hard to support very convincingly, there is no particular reason to think that the private level of saving in the absence of government intervention will generally be optimal (Samuelson 1983, 284–85). Thus, the government may want to nudge national saving either higher or lower, and can try to do so through retirement plan funding decisions.

Evaluating the Funding of Different Types of Retirement Plans

Social Security is often called a pay-as-you-go retirement system, since annual tax collections come closer to equaling annual benefit payments than to fully funding the system's long-term commitments. The typical next step is to contrast this pay-as-you-go system with one where the Trust Fund grows sufficiently to make Social Security actuarially sound as a stand-alone system for the indefinite future, thus ostensibly increasing national saving. This view, while to some extent defensible, conflates several different ideas in contrasting pay-as-you-go financing with full funding. Therefore, to help sort things out, let's start by considering a hypothetical Social Security system that would be completely pay-as-you-go and yet in a sense could be called fully funded.

Suppose Social Security consisted of an annual transfer from current workers to retirees, the level of which each year depended on how much the workers had earned that year in comparison to the retirees' investment profits. For example, if not constrained by considerations of real-world practicality, we might imagine a uniform head tax on each individual of working age that equaled 50 percent of the excess of all workers' average per capita income for the year over all retirees' average per capita income. The tax proceeds would then be divided by the number of living retirees, and an equal cash payment given to each. Lest the example seem too absurd, I should note both that it would provide arguably desirable risk-sharing between workers and retirees (Merton 1983, 327–28) and that other elements of the tax-transfer system could be used to adjust for earnings gaps between different workers and between different retirees.

This would be a pay-as-you go system that could be called fully funded—although perhaps not in common usage—notwithstanding that nothing had been set aside. By definition, future benefits would be adjusted as necessary to match future revenues, and thus running up a positive Trust Fund balance would serve no obvious actuarial purpose. (One could nonetheless imagine reasons for wanting to have positive advance funding—for example, to help finance the future retirement of a large age cohort that would do poorly under the per capita method.)

How would this system affect national saving? The answer is that it depends on factors that have not been specified. Although workers are forced to save, in the sense that they pay taxes during their working years and get transfers during retirement, the system might reduce national saving. Thus, suppose that people myopically base their consumption versus saving decisions on income for the current year. Then the fact that old people tend to save less at the margin than the young people whose money they get each year gives the program an income effect that reduces national saving. Or suppose instead that current workers have foresight but know that real wages are constantly increasing over time or that the young age cohorts that will eventually support them are relatively large. Then the fact that they expect to do well under the system when they retire may induce them to save less today, in a lesser version of your behavior upon receiving the $100 million bond.

This retirement program might, however, be criticized for its sheer open-endedness. Certainly, anyone who thought of privately operated retirement systems as providing a model that Social Security ought to emulate would consider its annual tax and benefit levels distressingly underspecified. Private retirement plans, with their reliance on enforceable arm's-length contracts, typically specify in advance either the "tax" side or the benefit side. That is, they generally provide a relatively determinate statement of either (a) what the employer must deposit in the worker's retirement account or (b) what the worker will get upon retiring.

If the private plan specifies what the employer must deposit in the worker's retirement account, it is called a defined-contribution plan. Such plans typically offer some degree of portfolio choice to the worker, who bears the upside and downside risks of how well the chosen investments perform. But a government-run defined-contribution plan could sever this link between who makes investment choices and who bears risk. Suppose, for example, that the Social Security Trustees made investment decisions for everyone, with benefits depending on how the investments performed.

Defined-contribution plans are often said to be inherently fully funded (Bodie and Shoven 1983, 3). While this would not be true of a plan in which you could direct the notional investment (for purposes of determining future benefits) of amounts not actually set aside, such plans are not the norm. Thus, the funding of a typical defined-contribution plan, along with its subsequent investment results, determines in full what benefits are provided. Under a private plan where you get the proceeds of your own retirement account and the investment choices were all available to you outside as well as inside the plan, almost the only possible effect on saving is to increase it. Being forced to save within the plan should either increase your total saving or leave it unchanged, and without transfers between participants there are no income effects.[3]

For a hypothetical government-run defined-contribution plan that might have income effects on saving, consider Paul Samuelson's famous abstract model of Social Security. In his model, real saving is literally impossible since all material goods melt like ice in a sauna, and thus, if Robinson Crusoe lived alone, he would die when he could no longer work (1958, 468). With succeeding generations, however, a tax on current workers can be used to support retirees. Now suppose that the retirement system uses a fixed percentage tax on wages and offers pay-as-you-go benefits. If everyone lives for exactly two periods, one as a worker and one as a retiree, and all age cohorts are the same size, retirees' investment return depends on the rate of productivity (and thus wage) growth. One might call this a kind of defined-contribution plan, since each worker's tax contribution is specified (in absolute dollar as well as percentage terms once current-period wages are known), but his or her benefit depends on productivity in the next period.

Strictly within this model—which many still regard, despite its extreme abstraction, as a "profound" justifying approximation for the current Social Security system (Ippolito 1999, 139)—national saving cannot be affected since nature requires it to be zero. Yet "everyone ends up better off" (Samuelson 1958, 480) from the system because it decomposes nature's zero-saving requirement into simultaneous forced saving by workers and dissaving by retirees.

Samuelson's model can be modified to fit a world in which saving is possible but not very productive at the margin because there is too much of it relative to good investment opportunities, and the interest rate on saving is therefore below the rate of productivity growth (Aaron 1966). In such a world, Social Security desirably reduces saving through its income effect on current workers, who need not save as much through their own efforts given the positive transfer (computed in terms of the interest rate on bonds) that they can count on receiving from future workers.

In sum, defined-contribution plans are by definition fully funded, but when run by the government they can either increase or reduce national saving if they affect it at all. Now let's consider the main private sector alternative, a defined-benefit plan, where the worker's ultimate retirement benefit, rather than the employer's contribution to the plan, is the thing specified in advance. With defined-benefit plans, we come to a case where the level of advance funding can vary. The amount that the employer sets aside may either be too low, too high, or just right to provide the amount needed to pay the promised benefits.

The greater the funding of a defined-benefit plan, the greater the saving within the plan itself. By definition, amounts in the retirement fund have been set aside for saving rather than directed to current consumption. We still would need to know more, however, to determine the effect on national saving. Suppose, for example, that a conscientious and default-averse employer adjusts its saving outside the plan to account for the adequacy of funding within the plan, thus potentially making the formal level of funding irrelevant. Or suppose that, the less adequate the funding, the more beneficiaries of the plan save on the side in order to assure themselves of retirement support. Income effects of the transfers in a government defined-benefit plan can further muddy the analysis.

Actual Social Security as Approximately a Defined-Benefit Plan

Within this framework of defined-contribution and defined-benefit plans, what is Social Security? One could say that it is both, since it specifies both taxes and benefits. Or one could say that it is neither, since (under the self-financing idea and the Trust Fund trigger) taxes are supposed to equal benefits over time but Congress has to decide what to do in the event of a financing shortfall. If payroll tax levels are politically sacred and benefits adjust as needed, it is essentially a defined-contribution plan like my rendition of the Samuelson model. If benefit levels are sacred and taxes do all the adjusting, it is essentially a defined-benefit plan and thus capable of being under- or overfunded.

In practice, while neither of these polar alternatives fully holds, Social Security is probably more of a defined-benefit plan. To be sure, benefits have at times been cut in response to financing concerns—for example, by about one-fifth in expected value to members of the baby boom generation through legislation adopted in 1983 (Kotlikoff 1992, 196). And from the 1930s through the 1970s, Social Security benefits were frequently increased, partly in response to the unanticipated revenues that flowed in to the system due to post–World War II economic expansion. If we thought the practice of adjusting benefits was sufficiently strong, we might say that Social Security does not so much have a financing problem as has failed to announce with accuracy its real future benefit levels.

To a large extent, however, currently promised Social Security benefits

are considered guaranteed. Or more specifically, they are regarded as important commitments that Congress should try to keep, albeit that hidden benefit reductions or those nominally outside the Social Security system (such as
by increasing income taxation of benefits) are not entirely off-limits, and that
increasing benefits (the upside of risk) may be a surefire political winner if it
looks fiscally feasible. Thus, we can meaningfully describe the system as underfunded given the long-term fiscal forecasts, rather than as simply having
issued overoptimistic advance projections of likely future benefit levels.

While Social Security is in this sense underfunded, it has not for some
time been entirely pay-as-you-go. Before adoption of the 1983 changes, it
came pretty close, with an official Trust Fund balance of under $20 billion
that was estimated to represent less than 1 percent of the present value of the
system's long-term gross liability for benefits (Smetters 1999, 202). But by
the end of 1998 the Trust Fund was credited with a balance of $681.6 billion.
This reflected a deliberate policy decision to increase current funding in response to the long-term picture. And to increase people's attention to the
long-term picture, Social Security's Board of Trustees annually provides
seventy-five-year forecasts, testing for "close actuarial balance" (defined as
95 to 105 percent of exact Trust Fund adequacy to pay benefits) throughout
this period. The lack of such balance is supposed to indicate a need for cor-
rective legislation (Goss 1999, 27), although it triggers no legal sanction akin
to the benefit cutoff that would result from exhausting the Trust Fund.

How does Social Security affect national saving? This is one of the great
disputes in modern econometrics, but the effect of underfunding on national
saving is fairly clear-cut. Martin Feldstein (1974; 1996) has long argued that
on balance Social Security reduces national saving due to the income effect
of providing transfers to older age cohorts, thus reducing their saving during
their working years (like the recipient of the $100 million retirement bond)
while the younger age cohorts that will finance the transfers are not yet able
to make savings decisions. This consequence of the income effect is generally accepted. It is also common ground in the empirical dispute, however,
that national saving is to some extent increased by Social Security's inducing
earlier retirement. All else equal, reducing your anticipated working years
and increasing your retirement years should induce you to save more per
year of work. Thus, the empirical dispute about Social Security's net impact
on national saving simply concerns which of these two effects is the greater
(Feldstein 1998, 10–11).

Only the truly fanatical fans of increasing saving at all costs should welcome the retirement effect. Driving able and willing workers out of the

workplace through the threat of reducing their benefits (in effect, imposing a marginal tax rate on their earnings that is far above the norm) should hardly be cause for satisfaction.[4] But in any event, the effects of inducing early retirement are beside the point if we are focusing just on the funding question and its significance for national saving.

Since the mechanism by which Social Security's underfunding has reduced national saving is its transferring wealth to older age cohorts from younger ones, people who want to increase national saving should probably focus directly on the generational issue. Taking money away from current generations, such as through immediate Social Security tax increases or benefit reductions that are not offset elsewhere in the federal budget, would be a straightforward way of shifting consumption opportunities to the future (the whole point of saving), whether or not it would be good distributional policy. Such measures would also tend to increase the Social Security Trust Fund as they took effect and reduce the degree to which the system is underfunded.

But since proposing tax increases and benefit cuts to the very voters who would bear them is bad manners and worse career planning for a politician or pundit, there is a widespread taste for more decorous ways of increasing Social Security's reported funding. And once the issue is posed primarily in terms of Social Security funding rather than effects on national saving, the public debate in large part turns into one about accounting rather than economics. Simply stating a higher Trust Fund balance automatically increases the system's funding as measured, although devoid of real effects except insofar as people (as in the case of the Cowardly Lion's medal for bravery) respond by acting as if it matters. And this presumably is fine from the perspective of anyone who just wants to reassure current voters about their future benefits, rather than to affect national saving.

There are, however, informal ground rules concerning the announcement of Trust Fund increases that will be accepted as legitimate—just as, in the children's game Simon Says, you must ask "May I?" before taking three giant steps. In illustration, consider a hypothetical proposal that benefit payouts to people whose names begin with the letters A through J should no longer count against the Social Security Trust Fund. Even if formally adopted through authoritative legislation, this proposal might appear too irregular and eccentric to create the stable new reality (where benefits are politically secure even without Social Security tax increases) that presumably was being sought. We therefore must look more closely at the Trust Fund, asking what it really is in practice, what if any implications for its proper computation can be derived from the underlying philosophy of self-financing, and what main ways of increasing it are on the public agenda.

Is the Social Security Trust Fund a "Fraud"?

Again, the Trust Fund's fundamental legal significance is as a trigger mechanism, since its exhaustion would require congressional action to keep benefit checks flowing. It is, however, thought to provide meaningful information about both the past and the future. Its assumed content about the past concerns the extent to which Social Security taxes actually pay for (in the sense of equaling) Social Security benefits. Its assumed content about the future concerns the economic and political sustainability of currently projected or even increased benefits.

With regard to the Trust Fund's effect on sustainability, some people may think that benefits actually come out of the Trust Fund in the same way that the ingredients for dinner come out of the pantry. Others respond by referring to "Trust Fund fraud" (Ferrara and Tanner 1998, 42) because the money that is reported to be in the Trust Fund is not actually there but has been spent. Both views require correction.

Perhaps a good way to start clearing up our thinking about the Social Security Trust Fund is to return to the private versus public comparison. However, given the imagery that the term "trust fund" naturally evokes, perhaps we should now compare what Social Security has to a private trust fund—the sort that finances the golden lives of people you may have only heard about, or perhaps (as I did) observed from afar as college classmates. These are the people who spend their weekends jetting off to ski resorts rather than trudging to Toys "R" Us or Burger King, and the trust funds their forefathers established apparently pay the tab. My own favorite close encounter with such a child of fortune concerned a college classmate—let's call him "Baxter" to protect the innocent—who was widely noted for speaking like an English novel and carrying an umbrella if there was a cloud in the sky. Perhaps his great-grandfather had cornered the market in pig iron. Asked if he was going to Paris for the summer, Baxter ("Bax" to his friends) languidly replied, "Oh, if I have the energy." When I overheard this, I had already begun my summer sentence as a file clerk in the bowels of a federal immigration office.

Baxter undoubtedly was a trust fund beneficiary. How did his source of support compare to the Social Security Trust Fund? Let's start by slogging through a short description of the latter, from an official publication of the Ways and Means Committee:

Contrary to popular belief, Social Security taxes are not deposited into the Social Security Trust Funds. They flow each day into thousands of depository accounts maintained by the government with financial institutions across the country . . . [and] become part of the government's operating cash pool. . . . In effect, once these taxes are received, they become indistinguishable from other moneys the government takes in. They are accounted for separately through the issuance of Federal securities to the Social Security Trust Funds—which basically involves a series of bookkeeping entries by the Treasury Department—but the trust funds do not themselves receive or hold money. They are simply accounts. . . . Simply put, these balances, like those of a bank account, represent a promise that, if needed to pay Social Security benefits, the government will obtain resources in the future equal to the value of these securities. (1996, 71)

What a sham, you might initially feel inclined to say. How dare they siphon off the earmarked Social Security taxes and leave behind nothing but empty IOUs? If such outrage is rightly directed, however, then it poses the question "What about Baxter's trust fund?" There, too, no pot of money is likely to be sitting in a discrete place. Rather, the trustees may have handed large gobs of it to financial institutions around the country, which in turn commingle it with the funds sent to other borrowers, and hand back pieces of paper that purport to state account balances that they promise to honor. Perhaps Baxter's trust fund also holds stocks and bonds that can be sold in the market for ready cash. But then again, the Social Security Trust Fund holds government bonds—not an optimal portfolio mix if this is how we choose to think about it, but certainly no sham asset in the marketplace.

Let's approach the question of what the Trust Fund means from a different angle. Would we be better off as Social Security beneficiaries if it held the tax revenues in its own bank account? It is hard to see why this would make any difference. The only things that really matter, so far as the government's ultimate ability to pay the benefits is concerned, are (a) having a large economy from which to collect any needed tax revenues, a point that is related to the level of national saving, and perhaps (b) having a sufficiently favorable ratio of government assets and expected revenues to government liabilities and expected outlays, as a way of ensuring that no dramatic and perhaps politically awkward change in ongoing tax and spending policy is needed to come up with the money.

Baxter's trust fund is different after all, but not by reason of using sounder banking practices. Rather, his fund faces default risk (it cannot print money or levy taxes) that it wards off through enforceable contracts between arm's-length parties. The situation for Social Security Trust Fund beneficiaries is both better and worse. They can potentially summon all the powers of government to ensure that their benefits are paid, and perhaps to alter the standing deal to their advantage. However, if the political winds shift sufficiently, then no positive Trust Fund balance or practice of sequestering moneys will help them.

Is There a "Right" Way to Measure the Social Security Trust Fund?

Again, notwithstanding the economic and political forces that will affect Social Security in any event, the Trust Fund really does matter to the extent that people act as if it matters. However, their willingness to treat it as mattering may depend on its being computed under rules that reflect some understood set of underlying principles. These presumably reflect its fundamental purpose of helping Congress and the trustees to administer what people agree should be (at least in the main) a self-financing system.

The self-financing aim goes back to Social Security's origins and remains important today. President Franklin Delano Roosevelt famously explained his insistence on it as follows: "We put those payroll contributions there so as to give the contributors a legal, moral, and political right to collect their pensions. . . . With those taxes in there, no damn politician can ever scrap my social security program" (Miron and Weil 1997, 11).

The Trust Fund keeps tabs on the self-financing claim to help make it credible on a systemwide basis. In effect, the theory goes, retirees are collectively entitled to the particular money that our records show they collectively put there. Only this formula's political saliency could make it a sensible commitment. It is one thing to say—as Social Security does not to the extent of its internal transfers—that I am entitled to get back the value I contributed. (Of course, even this suffers from looking at a mere subset of total taxes, transfers, and other interactions with the government.) Yet why should my degree of entitlement via Social Security have anything to do with what other people, to a large extent in different eras, paid in and got back from the system? To view this as morally significant resembles feeling on a deep emotional level that, on the days when I wear a blue shirt, the service I get in a restaurant should depend on the tips left there by other people who were wearing blue shirts.

Still, given the apparent political salience of a systemwide self-financing norm, the Trust Fund can have genuine importance as a precommitment device that has some likelihood of shaping—one hopes for the better, not the worse—future political decisions. The idea President Roosevelt had in mind may have been that the government cannot operate a credible retirement system on which people will rely if it is liable to renege at any time. Now, the extent to which reliance is desirable can certainly be debated (readers can get a much fuller account of the general issues it poses in Shaviro 2000). In my earlier example of the gratuitous $100 million gift bond, we might hope that neither the recipient nor future voters would regard it as a serious commitment. Yet if forced saving and retirement support are good policy, then we may want political barriers that will discourage the government from reneging down the line.

These days, retirees' fearsome political power makes the presence of a Social Security Trust Fund essentially coals to Newcastle so far as protecting their interests against those of other claimants in distributional policy is concerned. Just think of all the political scare campaigns concerning Social Security and Medicare benefits that have succeeded through the years. This reflects the enormous political power that retirees derive from their extra free time (Shaviro 1997a, 142; Mulligan and Sala-i-Martin 1999a) and their "single-minded" focus on government benefits (Mulligan and Sala-i-Martin 1999b, 12). Arguably, therefore, the real potential of the Trust Fund to serve as a political constraint that improves the likely content of future decisions lies on the upside, not the downside. The fact that Social Security benefits are already underfunded, if we think of them as required to come out of the Trust Fund, may tend to discourage unduly increasing them. Rudolph Penner, the former director of the Congressional Budget Office, notes that this consideration has "served to discipline the program in the past" (Murray 1999, A-1).

Suppose we take it as given that the self-financing norm for Social Security is politically valuable, and that the Trust Fund thus plays a useful role as the instrument for measuring compliance with this norm over time. Is there in general a "correct" way to make Trust Fund computations? Many people seem to think that there is, and they are not entirely wrong since self-financing is not a completely vacuous concept. This is why, for example, it would seem odd to disregard for Trust Fund purposes all benefit payouts to people whose names begin with A through J.

Yet there are real limits to the definability of self-financing. In a world where many things affect other things, what exactly does it mean for a program to pay for itself? This is not just a matter of taxes and benefits. We take it for granted that Social Security's reasonably measured administrative costs should be charged against the Trust Fund. But should the system be credited with lowering the riskless interest rate on government bonds by contributing significantly to demand? If the Trust Fund got into the stock market and the riskless rate therefore had to increase, should this extra cost for all newly issued government debt be charged against it? When the government intermingles all its funds anyway, is there any right way to determine which of its financial assets, earning varying rates of return due to risk or issue date, should be deemed to belong to the Trust Fund?

Even economists who ought to know better sometimes write as if questions of this kind had an answer. Thus, Martin Feldstein and Andrew Samwick assert that if a privatized Social Security system funneled money into the stock market, it would be "reasonable and fair" to credit the system not only with the after-tax profits, but also with corporate and property taxes paid on the underlying investments (1998, 221). They do not mention the usual economists' credo that fairness pertains to the treatment of people, not fiscal systems or books of account.

The main contemporary example of counting for Trust Fund purposes something other than Social Security tax receipts, benefit payouts, and officially measured interest receipts and administrative costs reflects a political compromise that was adopted in 1983. As part of that year's effort to improve Social Security financing, a portion of benefits was newly subjected to inclusion in the federal income tax. While politicians debated (and have continued to debate) the empty question of whether such inclusion is really a tax increase or a benefit cut, they agreed that certain income tax revenues attributable to the inclusion should be counted in the Trust Fund.

This had the arguable political virtue of permitting a kind of means-testing for benefits to be adopted by the back door and without the political penalty of being treated worse for Trust Fund purposes than a direct benefit reduction. Yet the decision was unavoidably question-begging if one naively thinks of it as more "correct" from the self-financing perspective than not so crediting the Trust Fund. Should the Trust Fund also be credited with income tax revenues from including the worker's share of the Social Security tax in taxable income? Should it instead be debited with the income tax revenue loss from not including the employer share in the worker's taxable income, when economists tell us that the two portions are identical in economic incidence? The only sensible way to address such questions is to ask how we want to influence future Social Security benefit decisions via the Trust Fund. Self-financing is at best a very rough means to this end, not an end in itself that is either fully definable or desirable for its own sake.

Prominently Discussed Methods (Apart from Tax and Benefit Changes) for Augmenting the Social Security Trust Fund

Since the projected long-term inadequacy of the Social Security Trust Fund is the main reason for the system's current prominence in political debate, the bountiful supply of proposals to augment the Trust Fund relative to its obligations should come as no surprise. Among the proposals are some to increase Social Security taxes and/or reduce Social Security benefits. These, however, while self-evidently augmenting the Trust Fund, would also have real effects that are better left for chapter 6, where I discuss "traditionalist" approaches to Social Security reform.

Two other main approaches to increasing the Trust Fund without so uncouthly (or at least overtly) handing anyone a bill have attracted even more attention. The first goes by the name of "investing" a portion of projected annual budget surpluses in the Trust Fund. The second is also called "investing"—the word must score well with voter focus groups—but here it pertains to moving a portion of the Trust Fund into the stock market. Let's take a preliminary look at how to think about these two proposals.

"Investing" a Portion of the Annual Budget Surplus in the Trust Fund

President Clinton first gave prominence to this proposal, which can be illustrated as follows. Suppose Congress decides that half of the projected budget surplus for 2002 should be "invested" in Social Security. Official budget forecasts then come out, estimating that the 2002 surplus will stand at $86 billion. To implement the "investment" policy, federal bonds in the amount of $43 billion (half of the projected surplus) are recorded as assets of the Social Security Trust Fund, thus increasing the Fund's official positive balance by that amount. The "investment" is also treated as a current expenditure of $43 billion for purposes of officially measuring the budget surplus. Thus, suppose the surplus, disregarding this transaction, ends up equaling $75 billion. (Perhaps income tax revenues fell short of expectations.) It is reduced by reason of the notional $43 billion transfer to the Trust Fund, leaving it at an officially reported level of $32 billion.

What is really going on here behind, or more precisely as a result of, these bookkeeping entries? As we will see shortly, Cowardly Lion effects on political behavior may be at the proposal's heart. But I will begin by taking the proposal at its rhetorical face value, rather than as an indirect way of accomplishing more sophisticated aims.

From a rhetorical standpoint, the proponents are (if nothing else) creative in using the word "invest" to describe a mere bookkeeping entry. If simply declaring the Social Security Trust Fund to be higher by some arbitrarily denominated amount really constitutes "investment," even if this is accompanied by one arm of the federal government's issuing extra interest-bearing securities to another arm, then we can all invest at home by writing ourselves billion-dollar, self-owed IOUs that we then "deposit" in our own self-issued "bank accounts."

Perhaps even more comical than calling the proposal "investment" was the political debate that it swiftly generated. Republicans charged President Clinton with duplicitous "sleight of hand" (Feldstein 1999a, A-20) and more specifically double-counting portions of the budget surplus that had already been included once in the Trust Fund. His supporters responded by pointing out the Republicans' double standard in charging double-counting and with convoluted explanations of how, if you do the right kind of "modified unified budget accounting," his proposal was not misleading after all (Aaron 1999).

The double-counting issue is worth clearing up before we turn to what the proposal actually means in practice. The Republicans' point was simple. The budget surpluses that President Clinton proposed to "invest" in Social Security already include (and would be much smaller without) the excess of current Social Security tax collections over benefit payouts that are credited to the Trust Fund. Since this excess is already included in the Trust Fund, he was in a sense proposing to count them twice.

In illustration, suppose that the federal government does absolutely nothing in a given year except collect a Social Security tax of $1. It has no other receipts or disbursements, and the interest rate on all outstanding government bonds (including those held by the Trust Fund) is zero. The results include the following: the government actually has a dollar more than previously, the Social Security Trust Fund goes up by a dollar, and the budget surplus for the year is a dollar. Suppose we then decide to say we are "investing" the entire budget surplus in the Trust Fund. Suddenly the Trust Fund has gone up by $2, even though the government collected only $1. Hence the complaint about double-counting.

The thought that occurred to me upon hearing of this plan was that President Clinton had lamentably failed to be as bold as possible in addressing Social Security's long-term financing problem. He could have "invested" still more in Social Security by proposing one simple change to the way budget surpluses are measured. Surely, he could have argued, all increases to the Trust Fund improve our long-term fiscal position. Therefore, computations of the budget surplus should treat it as increased by *all* increases to the Trust Fund—not just by those that result from net tax collections.

With this change in place, President Clinton could have left President Roosevelt in the dust as a Social Security visionary. Now, in the simple example I gave above, once the $1 budget surplus has been "invested" in the Trust Fund, the budget surplus goes up to $2 to reflect the full Trust Fund improvement. This gives us another dollar of budget surplus to "invest" in the Trust Fund, which now rises to $3. And this gives us yet another dollar of surplus to "invest" in the Trust Fund, which rises to $4. On and on it goes, permitting us all to retire immediately and enjoy, in the form of infinite, lifelong Social Security benefits, the wealth that our prudent "investment" has generated.

To explain what was wrong with this picture, the Republicans argued that any portion of the current year budget surplus that is included in the Trust Fund is not truly available to be spent. The whole point of crediting a dollar to the Trust Fund is that it will at least notionally be used to help meet our future Social Security obligations. To count it as free-floating and still unallocated (consistently with how politicians tend to view the budget surplus) is thus to propose counting it twice. The Republicans tried to avoid acknowledging that they, too, were proposing to count the same dollars twice, through their arguments that the budget surplus (including its Trust Fund component) showed current tax cuts to be affordable. They thus were willing to say that the same dollar was both paying for current government operations and going to the Trust Fund to finance future benefit payments—clear double-counting to the same extent as President Clinton's proposal.[5]

All this, however, concerns what one might call the proposal's aesthetics. Perhaps more important are its actual policy effects, which might prove to be significant, even though in a direct sense it is mere bookkeeping, given the political influence that bookkeeping can have. The main effects if bookkeeping turned out to matter would be twofold. First, by reducing the officially reported budget surplus, it might conceivably reduce Congress's propensity to enact current-year tax cuts and spending increases. This, in turn, would increase national saving relative to the case where the reported surplus was not so reduced if the extra tax cuts and spending increases would have been used to pay for increased current consumption. In addition, if the particular extra enactments that Congress would have chosen with a higher reported surplus were in fact bad policy, then discouraging them might tend to improve overall government policy.

As real (and perhaps desirable) as this effect on extra enactments might be, we should recognize that it lies in the realm of the Wizard of Oz and the

Cowardly Lion. A one-sentence statement by the president or Federal Reserve Board Chair, to the effect that the surplus should not be spent, would have the same effect if deemed authoritative. So might an arithmetical error by the Treasury gnomes who make annual budget calculations.

This is only the first Cowardly Lion effect of "investing" a portion of the budget surplus in the Social Security Trust Fund. The second effect comes from its increasing the reported level of the Trust Fund. If people treat the Trust Fund as significant in determining what Social Security benefits should be paid, then the bookkeeping change may increase the expected value of future Social Security benefit payments. In addition, it may reduce the extent to which Social Security taxes are likely to be increased in the future to pay for benefits. A good guess might be that income tax revenues would end up being used instead. This again is a real effect if the bookkeeping change causes it to happen, and one could certainly argue that it is desirable (for example, because the current income tax is more progressive than the Social Security tax). Again, however, a simple declaration by some public official about the desirability of using income tax rather than Social Security tax revenues to pay for unfunded benefits would have the same effect if considered authoritative.

There also is one final potentially significant effect of pursuing this two-part Cowardly Lion policy. That is the creation of a precedent for not requiring the Social Security system to pay for itself, and perhaps even for entirely discarding the self-financing idea. The Trust Fund may lose perceived significance as evidence of the extent to which participants have a "legal, moral, and political right" to their benefits if Congress is known to make arbitrary changes in the reported balance whenever it likes. This conceivably could hurt Social Security beneficiaries down the road by reducing public acceptance of their claim of entitlement. A more likely effect, however, might be weakening an existing constraint on increasing Social Security benefits, by showing that they can at any time be "financed" at the stroke of a pen by throwing extra government debt into the Trust Fund.

"Investing" a Portion of the Social Security Trust Fund in the Stock Market

A second proposal to increase the Trust Fund without changing Social Security's tax or benefit rules involves investing a portion of it in the stock market. Here the word "invest" has more reality, since the government actually would in some fashion hold privately issued financial instruments with a payoff that depended on how the stock market performed. This proposal raises enough important issues of substance, such as those concerning portfolio choice and the specter of "Social Security socialism" (Friedman 1999) via government stock ownership, to require fuller discussion in chapter 6. For now, I just set forth the proposal's underlying content and significance for funding.

It really has two parts. The first is for the government to engage in a set of actual financial transactions whereby it in effect swaps its own debt to the public in exchange for stock. No matter what happens to the particular government bonds previously held by the Trust Fund, every dollar that the government spends to buy stock requires it to issue an extra dollar's worth of bonds to the general public if tax and spending levels remain the same. The desirability of this debt-for-stock swap has nothing to do with Social Security or its financing problems as such.

Second, as a pure bookkeeping matter, the government credits the performance of its stockholdings to the Trust Fund. Here the expectation, given new force by a sustained stock market run-up but having broader historical and theoretical support as well, is that the return credited to the Trust Fund on its positive balance will increase, albeit also becoming riskier. Thus, unless the downside risk of stock market investment is realized, future Social Security benefits become easier to pay under the self-financing norm.

Assessing the likely effect on future Social Security benefits of the variance in stock market outcomes is difficult, because it depends on future political decisions by Congress. One way of thinking about this problem is to ask: Will Social Security in effect become somewhat more of a defined-contribution plan, where what retirees get really depends on how well the stock market does? Or will it remain primarily a defined-benefit plan, where they get what current law offers them no matter how the stock market does?

The latter alternative, or paying the same benefits no matter how the government's stocks perform, appears to be what proponents have in mind (Advisory Council on Social Security 1997, 86). Kent Smetters has noted that this means that retirees and older workers face no real change in their investment position through Social Security (1999, 208). The upside and downside risk really go to younger and future workers (assuming continued self-financing by the system), since their payroll taxes will go up less than expected if the stocks perform above current projections, but more than expected if the stocks perform worse. So far as stock market variance is concerned, these workers therefore face "an expected payoff equal to zero but with a risky tax rate" that presumably is costly to them given risk aversion.

Smetters is probably being too generous in accepting at face value the claim by proponents that the entire risk, upside as well as downside, goes to younger and future workers. A politically more plausible scenario might hold that retirees and older workers have some of the upside, in the sense that a sufficient increase in the Trust Fund might encourage benefit expansion. The widespread view that only reducing, not increasing, currently promised benefits is unfair tends to make stock market investment by the Trust Fund a "heads we win, tails you lose" proposition for retirees and older workers.

Could younger and future workers nonetheless benefit from government investment in the stock market that was attributed to the Trust Fund? Advocates insist that the answer is yes, based on the claim that the high yield earned by stocks relative to government bonds will permit future payroll taxes to be lower than otherwise (Ball 1998, 17–20). In part, their analysis is based on looking only at expected returns from alternative investments and ignoring risk altogether, which is plainly inappropriate when prices in financial markets reflect risk as well as expected return (Geanakoplos, Mitchell, and Zeldes 1999, 81). In addition, however, they may be claiming that stocks are a great investment that financial markets mysteriously underprice given stocks' true risk-return tradeoff over time.

This claim, while at odds with conventional economic assumptions about investor rationality and efficient markets, has respectable support in literature concerning the "equity premium puzzle" (Mehra and Prescott 1985). A number of different studies have concluded, after looking at a range of different assets and their performance over periods of time, that "the measured risk associated with equity returns is not high enough to justify the observed high returns" (Siegel and Thaler 1997, 194). This certainly might suggest an argument for the government to induce increased stock investment, and perhaps to hold stock itself and attribute the returns to the Social Security Trust Fund. The issues that this raises, however, go well beyond system funding, and I thus reserve them for chapter 6.

Summary

Social Security reform is on the political agenda due mainly to official projections that the Social Security Trust Fund, from which the system's benefit payments are nominally made, will start declining in 2015 and be exhausted in 2036. Exhaustion of the Trust Fund would have legal significance as a trigger mechanism, requiring congressional action to keep benefit checks flowing to retirees. In addition, operating an underfunded plan (as Social Security now is if we consider the benefits it currently promises to be real commitments) may be grounds for concern even apart from the slim chance of a future benefit cutoff.

People's concern about Social Security underfunding may rest in part on a misguided analogy between it and private retirement plans. If your employer sets up a defined-benefit plan that purports to offer you a specified level of retirement support, a failure to fund the plan in full (preferably through a trust that neither the employer nor its other creditors can invade) may prompt concern that the employer will renege or default on its obligations. In the case of Social Security, however, funding does not have the same significance. The federal government is unlikely to face involuntary default, may want to pay you even if it could renege (since retirees are a powerful voting bloc), and if it does not want to pay you cannot be forced to do so by the existence of a Social Security Trust Fund.

Nonetheless, Social Security's "true" funding level may matter economically if it influences the level of national saving, which many people think is too low. Historically, Social Security's use of pay-as-you-go financing in lieu of full funding has probably reduced national saving (even if other aspects of the system increased it) through the income effect of offering members of older generations retirement support that they did not have to pay for themselves. And while this is to some extent water under the bridge, adopting Social Security (or other) tax increases now would probably reduce current consumption and thus increase national saving due to an income effect in the opposite direction, if the rest of government policy remained the same.

Increasing the Social Security Trust Fund may not, however, be a valuable end in itself. All it really does is provide a bookkeeping record of measured historical compliance with the political aim of having a self-financing Social Security system. The Trust Fund does not actually provide financing in the sense that your pantry might provide ingredients for dinner. While Social Security's self-financing aim was originally introduced by President Roosevelt to ward off undue benefit reduction, arguably a greater danger today (given the political power of the elderly) is undue benefit expansion, which increases in the officially reported Trust Fund, especially if accomplished by mere accounting games rather than forthrightly enacting tax or benefit changes, might tend to encourage.

The two most prominent suggestions for augmenting the Trust Fund without tax or benefit changes are (a) "investing" in it a portion of projected annual budget surpluses and (b) having the government swap its own debt for stock and credit the stock returns to the Trust Fund. The former of these proposals is merely an accounting exercise, although it might have real effects in the form of discouraging current Congresses from adopting tax cuts or new spending programs, and future Congresses from making Social Security pay for itself. The latter proposal would actually alter the government's overall asset portfolio, potentially with important consequences, but raising issues that go well beyond this chapter's subject matter of funding.

6 Traditionalist Social Security Reform Proposals

Everyone agrees that Social Security must change in some respects, if only due to its expected long-term financing problems. While the changes that might be possible vary along multiple continua from the incremental to the dramatic, advocates of Social Security reform can mainly be divided into two main camps. First are the traditionalists, who mainly just want to improve the system's financial posture. Many of them would favor particular tax and benefit changes to rationalize or update some system features (such as those relating to married couples) even in the absence of a long-term financing problem. They are anxious, however, to "preserv[e] Social Security's fundamental character" (Aaron and Reischauer 1998, 96). I consider their approach in this chapter. Then there are the advocates of a specific bundle of fairly significant changes that they call "privatization," which I discuss in chapter 7.

Inevitably, some advocates muddy or split the difference between traditionalism and privatization. This is fair enough, since no one should feel bound by how the members of each group bundle together the multiple independent design details that they happen to favor. Rather, as in the old-style Chinese restaurant menus, we should feel free to choose some features from Column A and others from Column B. Nonetheless, I mainly observe a clean split between the two approaches because it is useful expositionally.

Significance of the Current System's "Fundamental Character"

What exactly is the "fundamental character" of Social Security that its advocates are anxious to protect? Let's start with system features that are not limited to the traditional approach. Social Security provides compulsory and nearly universal coverage. In addition, it offers wage-related benefits that, on a systemwide basis, bear at least a claimed long-term relationship to earmarked wage taxes and are therefore (misleadingly given the system's transfer content) described as an "earned right," unlike welfare benefits (Ball 1998, 60–63). Nearly everyone supports these design features,[1] apart from the suggestion (by traditionalists, not privatizers) that system self-financing be jettisoned via an injection of income tax revenues under the euphemistic guise of "investing" a portion of budget surpluses in Social Security.

More particularly to traditionalism, Social Security applies a flat tax rate and a declining-rate benefit formula to annual covered earnings, resulting in some degree of progressive redistribution unless high earners have sufficiently greater life expectancies. The tax and benefit rules are not explicitly linked. Thus, by making ad hoc changes to either at any time, Congress can change how people do under Social Security on a lifetime basis without being terribly overt about the distributional change. In addition, Social Security offers retirees no choice of benefit package, apart from early or late rather than normal retirement. The only benefit you can get is an inflation-adjusted life annuity with a wage-indexing component for the period up to your retirement.

These defining elements of the traditional approach permit a great deal of flexibility, as we should recognize if what we care about is end results rather than the fetishistic symbolism that induces so many people either to admire or despise the current system based on its historical associations. This flexibility suggests that, judged by any likely set of policy preferences, traditionalism offers ample room to make Social Security either a lot better or a lot worse.

Nonetheless, current Social Security's "fundamental character" is not entirely flexible or content-free. Let's therefore examine how it permits accommodating the main policy aims that a sensible government-provided retirement system might have. These are the three social insurance aims of inducing forced saving, limited portfolio choice, and progressive redistribution, and the possible macroeconomic policy aim of affecting (and for most current commentators increasing) national saving.

Forced Saving

Theoretically, any desired level of forced retirement saving by workers should be attainable through traditional Social Security (subject to the usual caveat if people can borrow against the expected value of their future benefits). All that is required to increase Social Security's forced saving element is an increase in benefits, financed by a tax increase on the beneficiaries if the system's transfer content is not being changed.

National Saving

Jumping ahead to the possible macroeconomic policy aim of increasing national saving, this, too, is at least theoretically attainable through the traditional system. Increased Social Security taxes would do the trick so long as they did not prompt tax cuts or increased government spending on current consumption outside the system. Nothing about Social Security's traditional structure affirmatively requires that it be underfunded and transfer wealth from future to current generations.

The main argument that Social Security's current approach is inherently unfriendly to national saving rests on a claim about the likely political effects of having a positive Trust Fund balance that is not reported as belonging dollar-by-dollar to particular participants. Arguably, a Trust Fund buildup may encourage tax cuts and spending increases outside the system even if (as seems to have happened in recent years) Social Security's long-term financing problem discourages dispelling the buildup through benefit increases. How to make a mere bookkeeping change that would actually change how Congress treats a funding buildup is hard to evaluate.

Portfolio Choice

This is where traditional Social Security really starts to limit the available policy options. The current system offers no choice apart from retirement date to people who do not have the resources and planning capacity through their outside investments to get where they want in any event. If you would prefer stock market participation, international diversification, or an inheritability feature to the fixed life annuity that Social Security offers, then you are on your own and possibly out of luck. In principle, the system could be modified to offer some degree of choice, but this might be hard to reconcile with calling the system a "traditional" one.

Despite the paternalism and moral hazard arguments for limiting portfolio choice, I personally find the extent and manner in which the system denies it hard to defend. Are Americans unable to make even such limited investment decisions as whether to accept a bit of well-diversified risk in exchange for a higher expected return? Why try to prevent people (in practice, only those who don't save enough on the outside) from trading the Social Security retirement package for something of equal actuarial value, perhaps selected from a short list of what are considered prudent options?

In addition, even if we continue to offer only one choice through Social Security, is the current choice really the best? Let's accept the mandatory annuitization feature, which helps prevent poverty at the end of one's life (and could be called an element of forced saving rather than of limiting portfolio choice). And let's accept as well the desirability of providing a minimum fixed payment to the elderly—in effect, a small annual demogrant that might, where feasible, be self-financed through forced saving. Yet these points do not rule out the possibility that retirees could benefit from being permitted or required to follow more venturesome investment strategies, above some minimum floor, in either of two respects: to determine the amount available at retirement to purchase a life annuity and to determine annual payouts under the annuity.

People who like the one-size-fits-all "defined benefit" character of current Social Security may believe it is the ultimate in risk mitigation for the elderly. However, in addition to perhaps exaggerating the extent to which risk mitigation (above some minimum level) should trump investor preferences, they may forget that if younger people who face variable economic circumstances are responsible for providing these fixed benefits, this is not really risk-sharing or even risk mitigation. It is simply risk-shifting from one age cohort to another, and thus hard to rationalize as social insurance.

Progressive Redistribution

Social Security's progressivity, or more precisely the way it smuggles progressivity into a setting of what are supposedly "earned rights" (Ball 1998, 60) that the beneficiaries have paid for, is perhaps its crowning glory to many traditionalists. Clearly, the extent to which it is progressive on a lifetime basis is readily adjustable. The relationship between the tax and benefit rules can be altered as Congress likes, and the ability to enact these changes over time provides a convenient tool for transferring lifetime wealth from richer to poorer age cohorts. On the other hand, the system's progressivity tends to be reduced (more or less invisibly) by not adjusting benefit packages for any actuarial measure of relative life expectancy.

The problem with pursuing progressivity through Social Security arises from the source of its claimed political advantage among redistributive tools: the fact that it is done in a relatively concealed and indirect manner. Departing from the traditional structure by having the value of your benefits, compared to your taxes, straightforwardly depend on your lifetime earnings would make Social Security's redistribution more visible or at least more clearly separable from everything else the system does. But it might also help to reduce the potential for such dubious redistributive results as transferring significant wealth to high-income couples with one earner.

An added social cost of keeping the tax-benefit relationship in Social Security so murky is that it may unnecessarily increase the system's discouragement of work effort. Again, in making work decisions, people may often err in the direction of regarding Social Security as a "pure tax" on work (Kotlikoff and Sachs 1997, 17) rather than as a wage tax followed by a wage subsidy. Greater public understanding of the relationship between current earnings and future benefits might reduce the adverse incentive effect even if the system's policy content remained the same. And while in principle this merely calls for better publicizing the relationship between earnings and expected Social Security benefits, a more forthrightly stated tax-benefit relationship might be helpful or even indispensable to this effort.

Perhaps all these costs of concealing the details of Social Security's progressivity are worth the political advantages that are attained thereby (assuming you like a bit of extra progressivity). How great are the political advantages, however? This is hard to say. We should perhaps be skeptical of the extent to which concealment actually helps. The claim is that we gull the middle class into supporting aid for the poor by folding all the benefits into the same program. But how confident should we be that the program, once predominantly tailored to serve middle-class interests, will really do more for the poor—taking into account the needy young as well as the old—than could have been accomplished more directly?

While readers may form their own conclusions, to my mind a traditional Social Security system is significantly flawed by its denying portfolio choice, offering what may not be the best portfolio choice, and lacking a well-specified relationship between individuals' taxes and benefits. Still, in some respects it is a flexible tool, and at present (but perhaps indefinitely) it is the only Social Security system we have. Traditionalist reform proposals to modify Social Security and improve its financing—along with proposals to modify the spousal rules, which concern many traditionalists independently of the financing issue—are therefore worth examining in general terms.

A word to the wise: Readers who are not interested in Social Security micro-details, and who thus skipped much of chapter 2, may want to jump ahead here to page 113, concerning traditionalist proposals to invest a portion of the Trust Fund in the stock market.

Proposed Tax and Benefit Changes

Traditionalist Social Security reformers have proposed a number of different ways to improve the system's financing through tax and benefit changes. Naturally, each proposed plan has its distinctive hit list, and none of the plans is especially worth highlighting at this stage in the political process. Nonetheless, the plans have enough suggested tax and benefit changes in common to provide us with a broader hit list that probably covers most of what Congress will consider if it takes this route.

These changes go against the grain politically by visibly imposing costs on people (even if it is hard to tell exactly who and how much) relative to the status quo. Since they therefore are not an easy sell, proponents typically introduce them with a kind of two-step. First, if possible, they explain why a given change might be good policy even apart from Social Security's financing needs. Then comes an estimate (perhaps as a percentage of the system's projected long-term financing deficit) of exactly how much the change is likely to help. The procedure brings to mind the recipient of a birthday gift saying, "It's the thought that counts," but then checking the price tag anyway.

Obviously, I intend no serious criticism of proponents who offer both a justification and a revenue estimate for the adverse Social Security changes that they courageously propose. It is hard to see what else they can do—smile disarmingly and offer an admitted bad idea of wholly unknown fiscal efficacy? Nonetheless, there is a point to being suspicious about traditionalist claims to raise money and improve policy all at once. In some cases, a proposal's distributional effect (how it raises money) has little to do with its long-term policy merits. We can see this by reviewing the main items on current hit lists.

Raising the Normal Social Security Retirement Age

One could argue that the great increase in life spans since Social Security was adopted in the 1930s supports raising the normal retirement age. Suppose that the choice of this age is based on when an average worker is likely to have become frail enough to really want to retire if it is affordable. The increase in life spans suggests that this point may arrive later in the average worker's life than it used to. This line of reasoning might suggest that the normal retirement age should rise immediately from its current point, age 65, rather than dawdling until 2025 just to reach age 67. And it might support the adoption of an automatic adjustment mechanism to the normal retirement age (like indexing annual benefits for inflation) to keep it in some sort of constant relationship to life expectancy or some other measure of changes in senior health.

The distributional effects of this change may be just about right if increased life expectancy has no effect on retirement needs, in the sense that people live longer but need not be retired for longer. And it may even come pretty close if the age when work becomes too hard increases for everyone in about the same proportion to life expectancy. But if, say, retirement at close to age 65 continues to be highly desirable on grounds of frailty in some occupations, such as those involving physical labor, then the increase may work undesirable hardship in some quarters. (Which is not to say that it is just right as it stands.) In addition, increasing the normal retirement age is regressive (relative to lifetime earnings) because it reduces the duration of the progressive benefit relative to that of the regressive tax (Coronado, Fullerton, and Glass 1999, 28). This may be good or bad (depending on one's views about progressivity), but its merits may to some extent be independent of the retirement age question as such.

Eliminating Dropout Years in the Computation of Average Indexed Monthly Earnings (AIME)

At present, only a retiree's best thirty-five years are taken into account in determining the AIME on which benefits depend. Various commentators have suggested reducing dropout years by making AIME, say, a 38-year measure. Once again, this may be a good steady-state proposal since it would move in the direction of basing the system's transfer content on complete earnings histories. However, its adoption would reduce benefits across the board since your AIME can only drop if more years are included in computing the average.

A recent study by Coronado, Fullerton, and Glass finds that the change would be regressive because it diminishes (progressive) benefits relative to (regressive) taxes (1999, 26). This regressivity may be offset if high earners have more variable annual incomes than low earners (as suggested by Steuerle and Bakija 1994, 185) and thus lose relatively more from counting the extra years. However, Coronado, Fullerton, and Glass find that the "variability of earnings [between income quintiles] is not materially different" (1999, 26). One group that would lose disproportionately is women who had relatively short working careers, and thus earned little or nothing in years 36 through 38, by reason of their involvement in raising their own children.

How does the distribution of losses imposed on current workers by shifting to a 38-year AIME relate to the policy aim of basing benefits on something closer to a true lifetime measure of earnings? In one sense, the distributional effect does indeed advance the policy aim. The shift to fuller information about career earnings may improve the correlation between people's benefits and their lifetime circumstances. Yet the change's effect on overall progressivity is in a sense anomalous. Why should the fortuity of how wage variability happens to compare as between high and low earners at the 35-to-38-year range end up determining how Social Security's distributional effects are modified?

Reducing Spousal Benefits

Another happy synergy between policy and financing pertains to spousal benefits. As we saw in chapter 4, the current spousal rules have dubious distributional effects (even though some response to household size and the retired houseworker problem seems desirable) and may unduly discourage work by households' secondary earners. Accordingly, some commentators have proposed reducing spousal benefits in one way or another, and thus straightforwardly reducing Social Security outlays.

This approach differs from the prior two in that its distributional effects would reflect the logic of the policy change that was being adopted. Change the significance of marital status or spousal earnings for benefit purposes, and presumably you get the change in relative treatment of households that you wanted. Yet the choice of new policy should not be unduly driven by the distinct aim of reducing Social Security's fiscal gap. The spousal issues are complicated enough that I defer discussing them until the next section.

Increasing Income Taxation of Social Security Benefits

Another proposed change with relatively coherent distributional effects is increasing the income taxation of Social Security benefits. At present, only people with modified adjusted gross income in excess of certain amounts pay income tax on any of their Social Security benefits, but (as such income rises) the benefits ultimately become 85 percent taxable. Moving to 100 percent inclusion of benefits for people above the income floor would raise revenue even if it were accompanied by newly permitting these people to deduct amounts that simply reflected the recovery of the Social Security tax payments that had been included in taxable income (Aaron and Reischauer 1998, 107).[2]

Whether we call this proposal a tax increase or a benefit cut, it would allocate progressively the burden of reducing retirees' net Social Security benefits. If in general you like how the income tax allocates burdens between people in our society, then its use here is bound to have some appeal. Of course, the logical conclusion of this argument might be that the income tax should entirely replace the Social Security tax, or at least directly take on more of the financing burden (as might result, say, from "investing" the budget surplus in the Trust Fund). The precise extent to which the proposal causes the overall Social Security financing burden to depend on the distributional scheme of the income tax is in a sense arbitrary.

Increasing the Social Security Tax via a Payroll Tax Rate Increase or an Increase in Covered Earnings

Tax rate increases are generally among the most visible and thus politically unpopular ways of improving the government's budget picture. We therefore should not be surprised that most discussion of restoring Social Security's solvency through an increase in the payroll tax rate is by opponents of the current system. Thus, Laurence Kotlikoff and Andrew Sachs (1997) argue that this rate would have to be 50 percent higher to match benefits over time, and call other means to the same fiscal end the same "bad medicine in separate droppers" (16). Traditionalists typically propose only modest tax rate increases (if any) as part of a broader package.

In fairness to the traditionalists, even absent any perceptual considerations, their distributional aims might predispose them against increasing a tax rate that applies only to earnings below the annual ceiling. They have given somewhat more attention to increasing the annual earnings that are subject to Social Security tax. This plainly would have a progressive effect up to the ceiling, although still without further effects beyond that point. A million-dollar earner would still be taxed the same as someone whose earnings were right at the new ceiling.[3]

Other Miscellaneous Changes

Traditionalist Social Security reformers have also proposed a number of other ways of improving the system's fiscal picture. One possibility is to bring currently uncovered state and local government employees into the Social Security system, thus raising money because these people, like most in their age cohorts, would pay more than they would get. Forcing people to participate in Social Security as a way of getting money from them may embarrass advocates who like to portray the system as a sacred and valuable entitlement. Nonetheless, one could make a good case that the exemption, which reflects obsolete constitutional doctrine, serves no good purpose. Exempting them but not others who are similarly situated is equivalent to providing a tax preference through Social Security for certain types of employment.

Another common proposal is to reduce the inflation indexing of Social Security benefits. The only obvious reason for providing incomplete indexing would be to reduce the real value of the benefits over time, presumably to regressive effect as with across-the-board benefit reduction generally. How-ever, a prominent though controversial recent report by five leading econo-mists suggests that the Consumer Price Index (CPI), which is the measure the government uses for all inflation adjustments, actually overstates infla-tion significantly (Boskin et al. 1996). If a more accurate inflation measure would reduce benefits over time relative to using the CPI, then the aim of keeping them constant in real terms would indeed suggest adopting this measure, although the impact compared to overstating inflation (and thus increasing real benefits) would still presumably be regressive.

Improving the Spousal Rules within Traditional Social Security

Let's now consider how the spousal rules might be improved within the structure of traditional Social Security, treating financing constraints as per-tinent but not absolute. Traditionalists, along with those who assume that the current system is likely to be with us indefinitely whether for better or worse, have offered such proposals as the following:

Reduce the Spousal Benefit as a Percentage of the Principal Earner's Benefit

Aaron and Reischauer propose that the spousal benefit while the primary earner is alive be reduced from one-half to one-third of that individual's ben-efit (1998, 98).[4] The only rationale they offer, apart from noting defects of the current rule, is that this would "free up funds" without going too far in the direction of worsening the lot of one-earner households. (How exactly they determine that one-third is the golden mean remains unclear.)

This might be a good proposal if the current spousal rules were roughly correct in structure but simply a bit too generous. Scaling back the spousal benefit would indeed moderate its various controversial effects. The possibly excessive transfer to one-earner households would be reduced. The high-earning households within this group would lose the most in dollar terms—although this may be the wrong way to look at it since the low-earning households' equal-percentage loss of benefits might hurt them more. And secondary earners would not need to work as long before reaching the point where Social Security ceases to be purely a tax at the margin on their work.

But if making the spousal benefit a percentage of the primary earner's benefit does not make sense to begin with, because it is backward social in-surance that directs the most retirement dollars and the greatest overall transfers where the need is likely to be least (Steuerle and Bakija 1994, 208), then this solution is rather inadequate. Tinkering with a flawed principle still leaves you with a flawed principle.

Cap the Spousal Benefit, or at the Limit Provide a Flat Spousal Benefit

A second possibility might be to cap the permissible spousal benefit for high-earning couples (Steuerle and Bakija 1994, 214), thus creating a flat or uniform benefit for everyone who reached the cap. If this were for some political reason an exclusive take-it-or-leave-it alternative to the current system, it might be worth doing, given how it targets the extra transfer to the households that are least in need. But it really is best seen as stapling together two distinct spousal benefit rules: the current one until the cap kicks in, and beyond that a flat-benefit system. It thus invites the question of whether Social Security should simply generalize the latter and provide the same flat spousal benefit at *all* earning levels.

Under such a rule, if structured like the existing spousal rules, secondary earners would get the higher of the flat benefit and their own earned benefit. Yet this would continue the current work discouragement (through a tax that earns no extra benefits) until you cross over to receiving your owned earned benefits. That effect could be moderated by providing instead that each dollar of earned benefits increases your ultimate receipt, even if up to some point you only get a percentage of it plus the flat benefit.

Perhaps a better feature of the existing rules is that permitting a secondary earner's flat benefit to increase upon the death of the primary earner. Here, the point is that losing the decedent's retirement income may worsen the survivor's circumstances. Although there is now only one mouth to feed, there may also be lost economies of scale (such as in paying for rent and food).

A flat spousal benefit assures all recipients a minimum subsistence level. And the distributional effect of providing it is likely to be progressive if the extra taxes induced at the margin by the need to pay for it fall more on high-earning than low-earning households. One question to ask about it, however, is: Why guarantee a minimum subsistence level only to secondary-earner spouses, rather than offering it (in effect, as a demogrant) to retirees across the board? Secondary earners are not the only people who may reach retirement without enough covered earnings to provide them with adequate retirement support through Social Security.

Give AIME Credit for Years Spent Raising Children

Another possibility might be replacing the spousal benefit with a rule that in effect awards covered earnings for benefit purposes to individuals who stay home to raise children (Steuerle and Bakija 1994, 214). If everyone had the same deemed earnings per unit of time spent at home, this proposal would operate somewhat like a flat grant that was an add-on (rather than an alternative) to earned benefits. If instead deemed earnings depended on the beneficiary's earning power, presumably as demonstrated in other years, it would be more like letting people who raise children count less than their thirty-five best years to determine their AIME.

One point to keep in mind about this proposal is that, like a spousal benefit, it would reward staying home and raising children relative to entering the labor market. Workers in the labor market don't just earn retirement benefits; they also pay income and Social Security taxes. Staying at home is therefore generally favored by the tax-transfer system even for those who get no retirement benefits. We may tend to think it unfair, not just regrettable (and at odds with good social insurance), for stay-at-home spouses to receive no Social Security benefits in old age. Yet we should keep in mind the distinction between the case for adequate forced saving by these people's households on their behalf and that for giving them a transfer because they chose to stay out of the formal labor market.

Levy Higher Taxes in Exchange for Higher Retirement Benefits

Whether or not the current spousal benefit rules rightly allocate forced saving between households, they are mainly criticized for their transfer content. This suggests that the system could be improved by levying Social Security taxes on more of a household basis, to match how benefits are provided. In theory, this could be done in a number of different ways. One possibility would be to require, on income tax returns of married individuals, the payment of extra Social Security tax if only one spouse had significant earnings for the year. The secondary earner would then be given deemed earnings for benefit computation purposes that reflected the amount of these payments. Proposals of this sort have been little heard and may be politically unrealistic. Yet they should not be ruled out by traditionalists who want to rationalize the current Social Security system.

Earnings-Sharing

A final proposal to fix the spousal rules is to eliminate the spousal benefit but require "earnings-sharing." Under most proposals bearing this name, Social Security taxes would still be levied on an individual basis, but the covered earnings (for later benefit purposes) that any married individual accrued would be split 50-50 between the spouses. Thus, for example, "if a husband earns $40,000 in a year and his wife earns $20,000, each might be credited with $30,000 of earnings for Social Security purposes" (Steuerle and Bakija 1994, 214), on which benefits would later be paid on a purely individual basis.

Relative to the current system with its generous spousal benefits that are funded by a transfer, earnings-sharing would benefit two-earner couples (214). Relative to a purely individual system, one might expect one-earner (or unequal-earner) couples to gain, since the progressive benefit formula would now offer a higher reimbursement rate to AIME credits that had been transferred from a high-earning to a low-earning spouse. Any such gain may be offset, however, in the familiar case where the higher-earning spouse (typically the man) is also older. Under earnings-sharing, the covered earnings that were transferred to the younger spouse presumably would not being generating Social Security benefits until she reached retirement age (Aaron and Reischauer 1998, 98).[5]

The distributional effects of earnings-sharing depend on the system details. And evaluating them depends on what you think about household taxation in general (a subject that would take us far beyond the scope of this book). Perhaps the most clear-cut advantage of earnings-sharing is that it may facilitate dealing with problems of divorce (Aaron and Reischauer 1998, 98). While the current system denies spousal benefits for marriages that last less than ten years and then (to avoid unduly benefiting those married more than once) requires using one set of spousal benefits at a time, earnings-sharing just gives everyone half the relevant earnings from each marriage. This may have greater design logic, since it lessens the potential for a slight change in circumstances to cause a big change in benefits. And it may strengthen the position inside the household of a low-earning spouse—who now has the option before year 10 of leaving with Social Security benefits—while also causing high earners to share in the burden of providing their former spouses with retirement support.

Investing a Portion of the Trust Fund in the Stock Market

Traditionalist Social Security reformers have been quite forthright in urging tax and benefit changes (albeit often obscure ones) that they recognize are politically unpopular. But human nature being what it is, they might be glad if free money could be dug up somewhere and dumped into the Social Security system.

In this regard, the traditionalists are hardly unique. Indeed, privatizers, who need more money because they want to expand, not just protect, currently promised benefits, are if anything more avid seekers after free money. And neither side's advocates seem very interested in taking a hard look at the reality of the free money they claim to have found or in explaining why Social Security is the best place to use it.

The main way traditionalists hope to get free money for Social Security is by having the government swap its own debt for stock and attribute the returns on the stock to the Trust Fund. No adjustment to the Trust Fund would be made for the riskiness of the government's stock position or for any increase in the interest rate that the government had to offer on its bonds due to selling more of them. A sustained stock market run-up may have encouraged some people to imagine—no doubt mistakenly—that the Trust Fund can only come out ahead from the swap.[6]

Traditionalists intend that the debt-for-stock swap bring no change in the defined-benefit character of what retirees get through Social Security. Thus, retirees would not actually participate in the stock market through Social Security except insofar as stock performance had previously affected the taxes they paid during their working years. The underlying aim is simply to permit the Trust Fund to be reported as growing faster than when it is credited only with the interest rate on government bonds.

Given this aim, one might think the traditionalists would settle for legislation changing only how the Trust Fund balance is officially computed, without requiring any actual market transactions by the government. The legislation could state, for example, that each year the Trust Fund balance will be deemed to increase at the rate of return for that year on some stock market index fund. The only issue that such legislation would raise is how we want the government to keep the Trust Fund books, given that its bookkeeping methods can influence political decisions.

To make the illusion real, however, the government apparently must actually hold stocks. And more specifically in a world of Clown family accounting, the Trust Fund must appear to be the true investor within the government that actually holds the stocks. Thus, the traditionalists' desire for free money encourages them to endorse an actual debt-for-stock swap by the government, and thus to insist that the actual consequences of the swap would be negligible or benign.

How should we think about this actual financial transaction by the government? For convenience, I divide the possible consequences into the distributional and the allocative.

Distributional Effects of a Debt-for-Stock Swap by the Government

Let's start by pretending that the government is a distinct flesh-and-blood individual that can experience pleasure and pain. Suppose it walked into your office and, with an earnest yet winning look, beseeched you to give it invest-ment advice. If for some reason (brokerage fees?) you wanted to urge it to swap its debt for stock, two main arguments would be available to you.

First, you might say: "You own no stock? And you can borrow at the Treasury's risk-free rate? Unless you're incredibly risk-averse, you'd be crazy not to borrow and acquire some well-diversified stocks, thus giving yourself a substantial expected return if history is any guide. Now, there admittedly is systematic risk that stock prices will plunge for a while, but surely that just af-fects how far you want to take this game. Almost no reputable investment ad-viser would advise you to hold no stock at all."

But then the government might point out to you that it already holds an enormous position in the stock market. It collects income taxes at both the corporate and the shareholder levels. Thus, as corporate earnings fluctuate, so does its tax take both from corporations and from individuals who get dividends or generate capital gains by selling corporate stock. Even if the only change in the stock market pertains to expected future corporate earn-ings, the government begins participating immediately through stock price effects on capital gain realization, and then continues to share the profits over time.

To make the similarity between owning stock and imposing taxes clearer still, suppose the government simply levied a 40 percent tax on all properly measured economic gain, and that losses were fully refundable under the tax at the 40 percent rate. Thus, if any business earned a dollar the government would take 40 cents, but if it lost a dollar the government would give it 40 cents. This would be roughly equivalent to having the government own 40 percent of the business as a silent partner that played no decision-making role.[7]

As it happens, our tax system is not entirely like this. It limits loss deduc-tions and imposes income tax liability based on a set of complex statutory rules that often bear only a distant relationship, if that, to measuring eco-nomic gain. Nonetheless, the income tax system essentially gives the govern-ment a kind of ownership position that, from the standpoint of risk and return, is very much like owning a substantial portfolio of stocks (albeit that the government cannot sell its investment stake in a given company). You therefore were mistaken when you offered the government investment ad-vice based on the assumption that it has no current stock market position.

Undismayed, you turn briskly to your second argument. "Stocks," you say, "are grossly undervalued. They are a great buy that you should not pass up." Here the government cocks a quizzical eyebrow, and you draw its attention to the "equity premium puzzle," or evidence suggesting that, given stocks' actually observed riskiness over many decades, they may currently offer too great a risk premium and be underpriced. Indeed, even before the Dow Jones index reached 10,000 in 1999, a book was being rushed to market by a reputable financial writer and a serious economist under the self-explanatory title *Dow 36,000* (Glassman and Hassett, 1999).

If Glassman and Hassett are correct, then everyone should rush out and buy stock until the undervaluation is eliminated. Alas, even if as you read these words the Dow has reached 36,000, or for that matter dropped to 3,600, you should keep in mind that not everyone accepts it, and if enough people did the Dow would already be at 36,000. Other analysts of comparable pedigree (although worse recent track records from a 1999 perspective) have argued that even at 10,000 the Dow is a bubble market, reflecting irrational exuberance and sure to crash soon.

Here at least you have the government's attention. What you are saying sounds too good to be true. However, if it is true it might support the debt-for-stock swap that you are urging, even though the government already stands to reap some of the benefits via its quasi-ownership position through the income tax. Just because it already has a good thing is no argument against scooping up some more.

Now, however, let's finally notice that the government is not really a flesh-and-blood individual. Rather than itself experiencing what sportscasters call the thrill of victory and the agony of defeat, its gains and losses are passed through to individuals, such as taxpayers, residents, and government officials. Thus, the right way to think about the government's investment position is in terms of any pass-through effects on the overall investment positions of the people who really bear its gains and losses.

What, from this perspective, would really happen if the government swapped its debt for stock? One possibility, well-grounded in neoclassical economics although perhaps not in reality, is that absolutely nothing would change. Suppose you already have exactly the overall position in the stock market that you want given your wealth. If you are not at your preferred position already, buying or selling stock until you get there should be simple enough. For that matter, if you want a negative position in the stock market, you can go short (such as by promising to sell stock in the future) and thereby bet that stock prices will go down. Now suppose the government blunders in and disrupts the fine balance you have achieved, by swapping debt for stock on your behalf (in the sense that stock market performance will now affect your future taxes and benefits). Not to worry—by simply reversing the swap through an offsetting stock-for-debt trade in your private portfolio, you can get back to where you started.

Elegant though this picture may be, it probably does not entirely hold. Most notably, the 59 percent of the public that currently is not participating in the stock market probably is in no position to back out again via cunningly constructed short positions, even assuming a desire to do so. Indeed, the 59 percent may not even want to back out if all they are averse to is taking the plunge through their own efforts (which would entail fixed costs such as learning more about financial markets), rather than having a stock market position (Abel 1998, 16). Accordingly, insofar as these people (through effects on taxes and government spending) bear the consequences of how the government's stock position performs, they may experience a change in true financial position by reason of the government's stock purchases.

If the government swaps debt for stock and not everyone restores his or her prior portfolio position by swapping stock for debt, there is an overall shift in the financial markets. Relative asset prices will change if the shift is significant enough. For government and other bonds, interest rates may rise and the prices of existing bonds may fall. For stocks, the most intuitive consequence would be for prices to rise and yields relative to price therefore to drop.[8] Stated more generally, the riskless rate of return should increase while risk premia, at least in the stock market, potentially decline. (The effect on other risk premia is harder to determine if the current risk premium on stock is inexplicably high.)

Returning to the government's imaginary conversation with its investment adviser, we can now start to think about the consequences of the portfolio shift in distributional terms. The great unwashed 59 percent ends up with a riskier overall position and a higher expected return than previously, even though risk now pays less than it used to. And, although in fact they were already in the stock market via the government's quasi-ownership stake through income taxation and the like, one could certainly argue that they were not in deep enough. While I hold no particular brief for this claim, it is a respectable one. Many economists, while perhaps overlooking the 59 percent's indirect stock market participation via the effect of the government's revenues from business on their taxes and benefits, suggest that in not directly owning stock many of its members are being unduly and even irrationally risk-averse (Smetters 1999, 208).

Likewise, if stocks really are undervalued, the 59 percent would benefit from being dragged in to share in the gain from making a bargain purchase. Of course, this argument goes away if stocks are not undervalued (just as the first argument goes away if they are already making rational portfolio decisions). And if stocks are overvalued by a short-lived bubble market, the argument reverses: the 59 percent would be made worse off by the centrally imposed change in their investment portfolios.

Accordingly, from the standpoint of the non-stock-owning 59 percent of the public, there is a plausible argument that the government should swap its debt for stock. The argument depends, however, on accepting controversial claims about optimal investment strategies or the likely future price path of the stock market. Neither the irrationality claim nor the undervaluation claim can be made with enormous confidence.

Even if the 59 percent would benefit from a government debt-for-stock swap, one might ask: So what, if the other 41 percent thereby loses? Changing asset prices and people's relative positions merely reshuffles wealth rather than directly increasing it. However, benefiting current non–stock owners at the expense of everyone else might be considered a good policy result for reasons of progressivity. Non–stock owners are concentrated toward the bottom of the income distribution, and perhaps only kept out of the stock market today by the fixed cost of learning more about it.

One last hurdle must be crossed, however, before we accept that the above claims would support a government debt-for-stock swap. The government can also increase progressivity by making income tax rates more graduated. And we have seen that raising tax rates on business income is similar to an explicit increase in government stock ownership (leaving aside differences in loss refundability and between taxable income and the economic profits that co-owners would share). It is well-known, however, that raising tax rates poses efficiency problems. Is increasing the government's stake in business income through direct stock ownership any different? This is the allocative question posed by a government debt-for-stock swap.

Allocative Effects of a Debt-for-Stock Swap by the Government

Most people agree that raising business taxes generally has an efficiency cost, even if on balance worth doing for distributional reasons. We tend to think about government stock ownership quite differently, regarding it either as totally innocuous so long as a few "institutional safeguards . . . all but eliminate the risk of political interference with investment decisions" (Aaron and Reischauer 1998, 111) or else as the dreaded nightmare of "Social Security socialism" (Friedman 1999). Even the most sophisticated observers often fail to recognize the conceptual similarity between taxation and direct ownership, which suggests that the efficiency issues raised by these alternatives are also conceptually similar, albeit that in practice they may play out differently.

To develop the comparison between the efficiency costs of business taxation and government ownership of business, let's suppose that a private business is initially fully owned by the individual who manages it and does all the work. He has all the right incentives to do good things for the business, since he will bear all of its gains and losses. Then he sells a 40 percent ownership share to a silent partner who will play no role in the business apart from accepting that share of the gains and losses.

Presumably, the two of them will only make this deal if they think it benefits them on balance. It does, however, create a brand-new incentive problem within the business if the silent partner cannot observe everything that the manager does (for example, how hard he works and whether he engages in self-dealing). This is the fundamental "agency" problem of business enterprise. The manager performs his role partly as an agent of the silent partner, but may benefit from pursuing his personal interests at the expense of those that are shared through the business.

For the public corporations that play so large a role in our economy, the fundamental agency problem that results from separating ownership and control has been well-known since the path-breaking work of Adolph Berle and Gardiner Means (1932). This is not just a theoretical problem, but one of real-world significance with which the shareholders must cope. In general, they try to protect themselves through either voice (vote out the bums who are currently running the company) or exit (sell the stock). A hostile takeover of the company combines these two tools: current shareholders exit and the new ones vote out the bums.

Suppose we take a company that was previously wholly owned by the manager and transfer a 40 percent stake to the government. Assume for now, however, that, because of our concern about political interference with investment decisions, we require the government to be a totally passive and silent investor. That is, it can exercise neither voice by voting nor exit by selling the stock.

The agency problem that the government faces here is basically the same as the moral hazard problem that it faces if it imposes a 40 percent tax as a social insurance device to mitigate income risk. Either way, the manager may reduce his effort or engage in self-dealing because he does not care about the 40 percent profit share that he does not pocket. And the 40 percent tax is indeed a totally passive and silent position. The government does not get a vote in business decisions and cannot sell its position in an underperforming company. If this were the whole story, we would now have a startling punch line: for the government to buy stock is identical in efficiency terms to its raising the tax rate!

As it happens, the world is too complicated for this punch line to be true. What makes it a useful starting point, however, is that it would be true if the world were simple enough in the right way. Thus, the way to get a handle on the efficiency consequences of government stock ownership is to focus on the real-world complications that prevent it from being entirely true. These pertain both to the tax side and to the stock ownership side.

On the tax side, the government participation that we actually observe through existing taxes is *not* just a profit-share. It affects a lot of incentives wholly apart from working less hard or engaging in self-dealing. For example, the actual income tax burdens saving (not just work), discourages selling appreciated assets, biases choices between corporate and noncorporate investment and of corporate capital structure, and contains a rich array of special tax incentives and disincentives that affect (many would say distort) the allocation of productive investment in our society. Raising rates under our actual tax system tends to increase the magnitude of all these problems, in addition to discouraging work and inviting self-dealing.

On the stock ownership side, by contrast, the efficiency consequences of a government position may be mitigated by adding in real-world detail but (for the moment) retaining the assumption that the government will be completely passive and silent, using neither voice nor exit to affect business decisions. My simple story assumed that the government would buy stock from managers who otherwise would have retained 100 percent ownership. In fact, however, managers' stakes (including through stock options and the like) in publicly traded companies are unlikely to be much affected by the government's entering the market at the level implied by the aim of boosting the Social Security Trust Fund. Rather, the government would mainly acquire its stock from the general public, including through mutual funds and pension plans. As to this stock, we had Berle-Means agency costs before the government stepped in, and we continue to have them afterward. How they change in magnitude depends on the comparative oversight abilities, through voice and exit, of the government versus the prior owners of the transferred stock.

Much recent law and economics literature about corporations has examined the possibility that large-scale institutional investors, such as pension funds despite their own agency problems, might enjoy economies of scale and market power that enable them to perform an oversight function on behalf of shareholders generally. Pension funds run by state and local governments to finance retirement benefits for their own employees have indeed in some cases played this kind of role—for example, by opposing "poison pills" that corporate managers use to entrench themselves against the possibility of a takeover bid that might increase shareholder value.

Nonetheless, due to the specter of political abuse, traditionalist advocates of a government debt-for-stock swap generally insist that total silence and passivity (rather than the use of voice and exit) would be imposed on the federal government in its shareholder role. Voting rights with respect to the government's stock would either be eliminated by federal law or greatly diffused among fund managers.[9] And investment decisions would go entirely to these managers, who would be selected through competitive bids and required to invest in broad market baskets of stocks (Aaron and Reischauer 1998, 111).

Accepting this (for now) at face value as what will actually happen, it is probably best viewed as a plan to reduce shareholder oversight of corporate management. Giving a role to the fund managers who win through competitive bidding does not alter this conclusion. They are agents, too, and the government presumably leaves itself less discretion than a private investor to shift between them at will.

Accordingly, one could argue that the Berle-Means problem of monitoring the agents gets slightly worse once the government is in the picture as an owner that plays no monitoring role. On the other hand, there is no strong evidence that the level of shareholder activism, at least in its "voice" form without regard to takeovers, has a significant positive impact on companies' performance (Black 1998). And many people argue that, on one ground or another, there is too much stock trading by active investors who compete with each other to find the undervalued stocks first, or who in their ceaseless trading generate excess transactions costs or fall prey to fads.

Thus, if we assume the government will be a silent and passive investor in the stock market, any efficiency costs of its swapping debt for stock are probably far less than those of increasing taxes. The main efficiency problem is the prospect that the government will not be entirely silent and passive after all, but will instead use its voice and exit tools to further political aims rather than to monitor the performance of corporate managers.

Whatever restrictions on investment discretion Congress enacts, it can also overturn. Traditionalists seek to allay this concern by pointing to the Federal Reserve Board, which has authority over the money supply. "Despite the political sensitivity of [this issue], the Federal Reserve system has sustained its political independence for eight decades" (Aaron and Reischauer 1998, 111).[10] This is far from a wholly persuasive analogy, however. Politicians' reluctance to risk being blamed for the next bout of recession or inflation by meddling with the money supply (Shaviro 1997a, 98) might not carry over to Trust Fund investment. In addition, the temptation to meddle with the money supply might be far greater if it were disaggregated; that is, if Congress could decide "case by case how much money to lend, at what rates of interest, to each prospective borrower" (99). Deciding which stocks to buy is subject to a degree of disaggregation that would encourage political intervention.

Thus, even if Congress created an independent "Social Security Reserve Board" (Aaron and Reischauer 1998, 111), it might well get in the habit of issuing narrow directives. Perhaps it would start by barring investments in tobacco companies and gun manufacturers. Then, mirroring what has happened in state-run funds and those in other countries, Congress might start mandating, say, investment in low-income housing, local infrastructure, or companies that promise to build manufacturing plants in Rust Belt states that hold key presidential primaries. Perhaps, as happened recently in Texas with Disney stock, complaints about the morality of recent film releases by some subsidiary of a big conglomerate would lead to hasty dumping of millions of shares (Ip 1999). In a thorough study of investment performance by state and local governments' retirement systems, published well before the current Social Security debate, Roberta Romano concludes that "there are no practical solutions to the problem of political influence on public pension funds" so long as (like Social Security) they are defined-benefit plans (1993, 796). Others are less pessimistic but agree that the problem of political meddling is real (Munnell and Balduzzi 1998, 19–24; Angelis 1998, 303).

Accordingly, the prospect of increased government intervention in the economy via its stock ownership through the Social Security Trust Fund is hard to dismiss. Does this mean that the intervention would be bad? The fact that it would tend to lower the investment returns that the government earned and attributed to the Trust Fund is really not the main point of interest. The retirement benefits that Social Security offers probably would not be affected, given the system's defined-benefit character. And while the Social Security taxes paid by workers might be affected, this is little different from the fact that the public always foots the bill in one way or another when the government's various market interventions reduce returns to private investment. Consider tax preferences that direct investment to unproductive uses, or regulatory restrictions that dampen entrepreneurial effort. Someone must bear the burden of any lost output, and the government (considered as a separate actor) directly shares in the cost if a less vibrant economy generates lesser tax revenues.

Thus, the real question raised by the prospect of government stock market interventions is how they would affect its overall allocative policy. Suppose you favor tax and regulatory action against tobacco or gun companies, along with government spending on low-income housing and infrastructure investment. Then it is hard to see what is inherently wrong with pursuing the same ends through stock market activity (be it trading or voting stock) rather than by other means. The only sensible reason to forego what you consider desirable interventions through the stock market is the concern that, in the long run, the bad interventions will outweigh the good.

Politically directed government stock activity clearly would offer politicians an additional tool by which to affect the allocation of investment in our society. It also would offer one more potential tool for extracting campaign contributions from companies or industries that want favors or will pay to avoid being hurt. If you are Milton Friedman, you are quite right to view this as a dangerous new threat. If you instead support a larger and more active government, then adding a new tool to the government's arsenal may appeal to you.

Either way, if the government cannot entirely forswear politically determined market interventions, the allocative question of whether it ought to swap debt for stock turns on your personal view (it is hardly a matter for conclusive proof) concerning whether at the margin it ought to do a little more or a little less than at present, given how well or poorly it does what it does. But the distinctiveness of the "Social Security socialism" problem presented here should not be exaggerated simply because the government would actually own shares directly.

Summary

Traditional Social Security is in many respects a flexible system that could be modified to serve a variety of policy goals. For example, its forced saving content could be changed independently of its transfer content through matching adjustment to tax and benefit levels. It could be used to increase national saving, such as by increasing Social Security taxes if this does not prompt offsetting tax cuts or spending increases elsewhere in the federal budget. Its progressivity is easy to modify through nonmatching changes to people's taxes and benefits.

Less easily modified without an acknowledged fundamental break, however, is the system's outright denial of portfolio choice to participants. In addition, Social Security by design obfuscates its transfer content through the separate operation of its tax and benefit tracks. This may conceivably increase the politically achievable level of progressive distribution, by permitting us to describe robbing Peter to pay Paul as the exercise of "earned rights" by both Peter and Paul. Yet the reduced transparency has downsides as well, including needless work deterrence if people underestimate the accrual of Social Security benefits through work, and the possibility that bad transfers as well as good are encouraged by hiding the ball. Examples might include the favorable spousal treatment of high-income one-earner households and the relative generosity of transfer policy (through Social Security in partnership with Medicare) for the needy old as compared to the needy young.

Advocates of traditionalist Social Security reform have proposed a variety of tax and benefit changes to improve the system's long-term funding. Sometimes, there is little connection between the design merits of a proposed change and the desirability of its distributional effects. This disconnect is a direct consequence of the Rube Goldberg character of its multipart benefit formula and complicated tax-benefit interactions.

On spousal benefits, some traditionalists have commendably taken the lead in proposing reform without just trying to cut benefits by the back door. Unfortunately, the tendency of the current system to discourage clear thinking about the tax-benefit relationship impedes addressing the forced-saving needs of stay-at-home spouses without making what are perhaps excessive transfers to one-earner couples. Traditional Social Security is in principle flexible enough to do better in its treatment of household issues, but this will require clear thinking about the difficult choices that are involved.

Traditionalists' advocacy of Trust Fund investment in the stock market reflects the natural appeal of what at least looks like free money. They would like to be able to credit increased returns to the Trust Fund and often seem prepared to ignore any resulting changes in the Trust Fund's or the government's overall risk position. This change could be accomplished through pure bookkeeping by simply having the government credit deemed stock market returns to the Trust Fund. However, popularly accepted bookkeeping conventions might forbid such crediting unless the government actually swapped its debt for stock in the financial markets.

Such a swap would probably increase the true stock market participation of those Americans (59 percent, according to a recent estimate) who currently hold no stock. Given Social Security's defined-benefit character, the main mechanism for their effective participation would be through effects on tax liability during their working years of how the government's portfolio performed. These people, who are mainly concentrated in the lower portion of the income distribution, would benefit from the swap if, in fact, they ought to have a greater stock position than they currently do (even through the government as taxpayers and residents)—for example, if stocks are under-valued.

A debt-for-stock swap by the government also would invite it to influence the allocation of investment in our society through its exercise of voice (by voting its stock) or exit (by trading its stock). The temptation to exert such influence would be hard to resist despite various safeguards that have been discussed, such as creating a "Social Security Reserve Board" that was elaborately insulated from direct political influence. However, the merits of any such exertion of influence should be judged as allocative policy, not from the Clown family accounting perspective of its effect on returns to the Trust Fund. Ask yourself what you would think of expanding the government's influence on the economy via taxes, spending, or regulation, and you may well be able to discern what you should think about doing it this way.

7 Proposals to "Privatize" Social Security

What Does "Privatization" Mean?

Traditionalist Social Security reformers may well hold the high ground politically. The public's view that Social Security has done well in the past and its caution about tampering with people's retirement income may incline it to insist that the current system be retained, at least as a matter of labeling. Nonetheless, those who dislike the current system have at least one good card to play. They can note that Social Security fails to offer current generations an appealing rate of return on their tax contributions and offer to fix this problem by increasing benefits.

As we have seen, the complaint about Social Security returns reflects a wealth transfer through the system to older generations, rather than, say, incompetence in investing people's tax contributions (although the system does indeed provide no option to seek higher returns at greater risk). To an ill-informed public, however, a spurious cause for Social Security's offering a "bad deal" may naturally come to mind. Consider the fact that privately-run retirement plans, which usually offer portfolio choice and forego transfers between their voluntary participants, invariably offer a higher return to current age cohorts (and especially the more affluent members thereof) than Social Security. The contrast invites an invidious comparison—albeit a misleading one—between government-run and private plans, drawing on what we know, from decades of experience around the globe, about government versus competitive private production of various business and consumer goods.

Governments frequently do a bad job at producing various commodities—for example, operating a steel factory, making shoes, or managing public housing. Turning over such businesses to private firms that have a conventional profit motive often yields a large payoff to society if the firms face competitive pressures and meaningful market prices in an environment characterized by the rule of law (with property rights, contract enforcement, and non-extortionary taxes). In the right setting, therefore, "privatization," or replacing government ownership with private production, yields genuine free money of a sort through efficiency gains in production, greater attention to customer wants, and increased innovation. Accordingly, if Social Security provides current generations with a low return, what could be more obvious than privatizing it as well?

Obvious though this line of reasoning may seem, it is misguided. Social Security does not require economic production of a sort that governments typically cannot do well. All it does is transfer sums of money around, which governments are quite good at doing. Economies of scale and the government's vast experience in handling tax and transfer operations generally help hold down Social Security's administrative costs to an estimated 0.6 percent of benefit payments, or about $9 per participant per year (Mitchell 1998, 414). Some argue that the system provides poor customer service, such as in explaining benefits to current workers (Kotlikoff and Sachs 1997). And clearly it does not provide customer choice or develop innovative benefit packages as one might expect from a private business operating in a competitive environment. Yet "privatization" in the most obvious sense—turning over tax collection and/or benefit payment to commercial providers that must compete for customers—simply does not offer the types of gains that you might expect from converting, say, Soviet-style into American-style shoe production.

As it happens, the main advocates of the approach to Social Security reform that goes by the name of privatization have a lot more in mind than just letting participants use Wall Street financial advisers. They also propose various independent policy changes. In addition, they do not want to take the government completely out of the retirement business. Social Security, in most privatization schemes, would still involve forced saving and limits on portfolio choice. The term "privatization" thus is not entirely apt for the set of proposals that go by the name.

In determining what "privatization" really means, I should note that no one who uses the term can claim trademark protection. If you want to propose that Social Security give you a billion dollars, you can call the proposal "privatization" if you like, but the usage may not catch on. Still, while there is no single or definitive "privatization" prototype, the term is firmly associated with a set of proposals by the economist Martin Feldstein, who has championed it since 1995 and promoted extensive research concerning its contours.[1]

Social Security privatization in Feldstein's sense involves three substantive changes to the current system, with associated administrative and bookkeeping changes. The various changes are as follows:

1. A shift from an underfunded to a fully funded plan, motivated by the aim of increasing national saving.
2. A shift from a defined-benefit plan that offers only one benefit package to a defined-contribution plan that offers some portfolio choice, such as permitting different levels of well-diversified stock market investment.
3. The elimination of all transfers within the system, apart from any that result from paying off benefits under traditional Social Security.
4. A shift of various administrative functions, such as holding and investing people's tax contributions and paying out their benefits, from government employees to private businesses that are subject to government regulation.
5. A bookkeeping shift in how Social Security funding is reported. Money held by the system would no longer just (if at all) be reported as belonging to a collective Trust Fund. In addition or instead, it would be allocated to participants' individual accounts, based on their tax contributions and investment choices. Individuals might to some extent have vested legal rights to receive retirement benefits reflecting the value of their accounts.

It should be clear that these features are independent of each other and associated only by reason of the fortuitous policy preferences of leading privatization advocates. Feldstein agrees that a fully funded program could in principle be managed by the government, without requiring the other changes (1995, 4). Thus, Change 1 is independent. Portfolio choice could be offered at any level of current funding (although not in a defined-benefit setting). Thus, Change 2 is independent.[2] Transfers between participants could be maintained in a funded system and without regard to the availability of portfolio choice. Thus, Change 3 is independent. Administrative functions could be privatized subject to regulation or kept public no matter what the system's policy content. Thus, Change 4 is independent. Finally, bookkeeping is a flexible proposition, and we will see that some politicians have actually proposed adopting "individual accounts" in name only, while keeping 99 percent of the current system's substance. Thus, Change 5 is independent.

The independence of these features means that privatization should not be regarded as a single take-it-or-leave-it package. Rather, its features can be adopted or not in whatever combination we like, in addition to each being subject to considerable variation. Thus, the right way to look at privatization is not as a single, unitary alternative to the current Social Security system, but as convenient shorthand for an arbitrarily assembled bundle of proposed changes, each of which merits separate consideration.

Before engaging in this five-part inquiry, however, I will consider a politically important element of how privatization has been presented. This is the financing problem all over again, but magnified. Privatizers cannot seriously hope that people will heed their call for multiple, potentially unsettling changes unless, like advertisers on late-night television, they can offer the equivalent of a double-your-money-back guarantee. Thus, as a political matter they must promise both to protect all existing Social Security retirement benefits and to offer glittering new ones. Our already underfunded system must therefore be modified to offer full funding for all that it currently offers plus a whole lot more.

For this ambitious purpose, a small injection of free money is not enough. And the gains one might usually associate with privatizing industry, in the form of more efficient production, are not available here. The iron constraint of financial markets—the fact that it is hard consistently to exceed the market return for a given risk level or type of investment—continues to apply. Greater portfolio choice and improved customer service may be important, but they are not dramatic enough to serve the privatizers' political need for a large-scale financing improvement. Yet somehow a large-scale money machine must be found and activated. Privatization is therefore not for the bashful. As a political matter it requires a daring sortie into the undefended but as yet uninvaded realm of "money on the table" that is just lying there, unclaimed by anyone.

Money Machines and the "Transition Path" Problem

With Social Security already underfunded, tax increases or benefit cuts seem likely no matter what the future policy goals if no magical financing source can be found. The time when, as a practical matter, this would have to happen is unclear, but two dates to keep roughly in mind are 2015, when Social Security is currently projected to begin incurring annual deficits, and 2036, the currently projected date for Trust Fund exhaustion.

A decision to move promptly to full funding makes the financing problem more immediate. And if you want as well to offer enhanced retirement benefits without unduly increasing downside risk, then still more money is needed. Martin Feldstein and Andrew Samwick call this the "transition path" problem and note the widespread concern that addressing it would be "too costly to be politically acceptable" (1998, 216). Other commentators observe that a shift to full funding "would require the transitional generation to pay twice—for their own retirement through a fully-funded system, and that of the currently and near-retired through the old pay-as-you-go system" (Bosworth 1996, 100).

This common view of the problem could stand a bit of clarification. A description of current workers as paying twice gives undue significance to the details of Social Security's actual cash flow (or rather a stylized version of it, since Social Security revenues are not actually segregated from the rest). Recall my suggestion in chapter 3 that it is generally more illuminating to think of people as paying for their own Social Security benefits plus or minus a transfer, than to focus on which age cohort provides the actual funds that are transferred to another age cohort. In addition, the question of how many times a given individual is taxed has little independent significance. Most of us would rather be taxed ten times at 2 percent than once at 50 percent.

There is, however, potentially a straightforward distributional problem. If we increase taxes for current workers by swiftly shifting to full funding, then (all else equal) they will indeed pay higher taxes than older or younger age cohorts due to a fortuity that is unrelated to relative lifetime earnings.

In a sense, privatizers are being too hard on themselves when they link the "transition path" problem to their entire bundle of proposed changes. One could compare the dilemma they pose for themselves to a proposal to pay off the entire national debt and also fund a Star Wars missile defense program, leading to what the proponents might call a "transition path" problem of coming up with the money. So far as fair treatment is concerned, however, privatizers make it up to themselves by identifying supposed money machines and claiming the proceeds for their own proposal rather than someone else's.

Suppose we really could identify a multibillion dollar money machine—that is, a way of getting something for virtually nothing, and thereby increasing society's resources so greatly that the need to pay for moving to full financing would feel at worst like a mosquito bite. By definition, any money machine that we can identify is worth exploiting, unless you posit that the proceeds will be totally wasted or even somehow used to make things worse. (An illustration of this perhaps far-fetched possibility would be giving free money to Saddam Hussein.) However, merely identifying a credible money machine does not, without more, show that it should be used to pay for current-law plus expanded Social Security benefits. Pending further discussion, the money machine could just as well be used to send a team of astronauts on a round trip to Pluto. Or, to make the choice more politically realistic, it could be dedicated to increased spending on education or national defense, or on tax cuts for everyone, rather than on consumer spending by retirees.

The money machine that Martin Feldstein identifies is increasing national saving. This is not quite a free lunch, because plenty of people may lose from having their current consumption curtailed, but it is the next best thing. Feldstein and Samwick present extensive projections in which the pain of extra saving is greatly mitigated by their assumption that it earns as much as a 9 percent return (1998, 218) and yet only needs to be discounted at 3 percent (241). This is indeed a wonderful bonanza if you can find it. Most of us would be happy to engage in a lot of extra financial transactions that earned at 9 percent and cost only 3 percent (whether tangibly or psychically).

To the extent this opportunity to earn a substantial positive return actually exists, we should perhaps keep on exploiting it even long after Social Security's financing problems are but a dim memory. Whether it actually exists, however, is linked to the question of whether Feldstein is right about the strength of the case for increasing national saving. I defer this question for the moment, since it will come up below in the discussion of privatization's bundle of proposed changes.

Feldstein proposes to increase national saving through mandatory contributions to personal retirement accounts (PRAs) equaling 2 to 3 percent of people's Social Security covered earnings (Feldstein, Ranguelova, and Samwick 1999). The expected future benefits from cashing in the PRAs ostensibly would not reduce people's other saving outside the Social Security system because "the vast majority of Americans have too little in financial assets to do any such offsetting" (Feldstein and Samwick 1999, 8).

Both to make the proposal more politically palatable and to discourage other, possibly dubious enactments by Congress, Feldstein and Samwick suggest that the cost of making the contributions might be fully defrayed by refundable income tax credits to the contributors (1999, 8). If so, then what essentially would happen is a cash transfer by the government into what were denominated as individual accounts, leading to a reduction in the reported level of the budget surplus. The reason this ostensibly would increase national saving is that "in the absence of the PRA program the government would use the projected budget surpluses to finance various tax cuts and spending increases, bringing the economy back to budget balance" (8 n. 14) and thereby increasing current consumption. This, of course, is not a saving increase relative to that which would result from simply retaining the tax and other policies currently on the books. By this light, one could increase national saving still more by first announcing a tax cut that would cost $500 billion per year, and then calling it off to generate increased saving relative to implementing it.

The close resemblance between the privatizers' proposed bookkeeping maneuver and President Clinton's suggestion that the budget surplus be reduced by notionally "investing" it in the Trust Fund has deterred neither side from applying a remarkable double standard. Feldstein, despite his willingness to assume that his own plan would increase national saving by reducing the reported budget surplus that could be used to fund tax cuts and spending increases, argues that the president's way of doing the same thing "adds nothing to national saving" (1999a, A-20). Likewise, while Robert Reischauer insists that the president's Trust Fund maneuver "would boost our national saving" (1999, A-23) and Henry Aaron agrees (1999, 719), something mysterious happens when the two of them team up. Suddenly they are so skeptical of Feldstein's version of the maneuver that they call its effects in this regard "complicated and unclear," and in their "report card" on his plan give it a D for increasing national saving (Aaron and Reischauer 1998, 128).

The Bookkeeping Shift from a Trust Fund to Individual Accounts

Let's now turn to the substance of the multiple reform proposals that, as a package, go by the name of privatization. I start with the bookkeeping shift from just having an overall Trust Fund to attributing Social Security revenues and investment returns to participants' individual accounts. Some people may view this as a change in substance, rather than just bookkeeping. To the extent they are right, however, this merely reflects either accompanying changes in substance or the fact that bookkeeping, like the Cowardly Lion's receipt of a medal for bravery, can actually affect behavior.

Depending on what rigor we demand of the term "individual accounts," they may already exist today. Records maintained by the Social Security Administration permit it to keep track of individual tax contributions and to estimate the monthly payments that people can expect upon retirement at different ages if they continue their current earnings rates. An individualized statement containing this information is currently available to participants upon request. Fairly soon, "Social Security Statements" containing this information will begin to be sent to all participants at periodic intervals automatically. These certainly look like statements about people's individual accounts.

What distinguishes a "true" individual account from this? Several answers are possible. One might be that it isn't really an individual account unless you are legally entitled to it. Yet this implies, probably contrary to what people mean by the term, that legally guaranteeing benefits would by itself turn Social Security into a system of individual accounts. And legal entitlement is a matter of degree. Even as things stand today, Social Security benefits, especially for current retirees and near-retirees, are well-protected politically against the threat of significant adverse change. Moreover, creating an enforceable legal claim to benefits might mean less than meets the eye, since the government has ways of taking back indirectly what it grants directly. A good example relates to the income tax treatment of tax-favored employer-provided retirement plans that unambiguously have individual accounts. Congress enacted in 1986 (and repealed in 1997) a special 15 percent penalty tax on "excess distributions" from these plans, above and beyond simply treating the distributions as taxable income. While in force, this special tax effectively took away something to which plan beneficiaries had seemingly been entitled. The possibility of doing the same thing to "guaranteed" Social Security benefits means that they may not be guaranteed after all.

Another possible ground for arguing that the current system, even with more reporting, lacks true individual accounts might be that its transfer content is inconsistent with the idea. Yet few would regard individual account status as inconsistent with the occurrence of some positive or negative transfer at the contribution or distribution stage. The above penalty tax gives an example of a negative transfer from what are still considered individual accounts. An example of a positive transfer is provided by President Clinton's 1999 proposal that Social Security retirement benefits be supplemented by "USA accounts" outside the system, with government matching contributions for low- and middle-income workers. Does combining the two types of transfers mean you no longer have a system of individual accounts despite the creation of (at least ostensibly) vested legal rights?

Perhaps the safest thing to say is that whether someone uses the term "individual accounts" in describing a proposal should not be given too much significance. What really matter are the underlying policy features, including a system's transfer content, allowance of portfolio choice, and likely political risk. The pure bookkeeping element can, however, conceivably affect political risk, along with Congress's inclination to regard Social Security cash flows as relevant to the enactment of tax cuts or spending increases. Again, describing Social Security's current or historical positive cash-flow balance as belonging to a set of individual accounts, rather than to a collective Trust Fund, might conceivably cause Congress to view the funds as less available for other uses.

In practice, a further reason for caution about the use of the term "individual accounts" is that it can be used without regard to whether an account's stated balance will actually affect the nominal owner's retirement benefits. By analogy, suppose that the government sent you a monthly "Report of Individual Account Balance," nicely engraved with your name and suitable for framing, that stated the current market value of Warren Buffett's stockholdings. "Your individual account now holds $2.364 billion" (or whatever), the statement might say. And the small print at the bottom might add: "Not for actual distribution to you at any time." This, it is fair to say without undue hyperbole, would not be a meaningful individual account.

In the context of actual political debate, this example is not as far-fetched as it may seem. Several widely noted recent proposals have suggested creating individual accounts, with a defined-contribution structure and perhaps some portfolio choice, that would only conditionally be used at retirement. A retiree would be guaranteed his current-law Social Security benefits, and thus would not use the account unless it was large enough to fund the purchase of a larger annuity (Gramlich 1998, 64). The accounts of retirees who ended up getting the traditional benefits would go over to the Social Security Trust Fund, thus improving its reported financing. In these proposals, the meaningfulness of the new individual account feature depends on the likelihood that it will actually determine (or at least affect) the nominal owner's retirement benefits. Depending on design details, this likelihood can be anywhere from 0 to 100 percent.

The extreme case of a plan for individual accounts in name only, since they would have so little effect on benefits, came in an unintentionally hilarious 1999 proposal by leading Republican congressmen Bill Archer and Clay Shaw. Under the Archer-Shaw "Social Security Guarantee Plan," people would be described as receiving a 2 percent tax credit on their covered earnings. They would not see this money, however; it would instead be deposited in their individual accounts. Each worker would then get to choose a mutual fund that would invest the account 60 percent in stocks and 40 percent in bonds. Gains would accumulate tax-free, and at retirement the worker would get the usual choice between traditional Social Security benefits and what the accounts permitted them to purchase. Congressman Archer proudly remarked that the plan "puts faith in the American people to make their own retirement investment decisions" (Donmoyer 1999, 608).

The punch line to the joke was that due to the individual accounts' limited funding (2 percent is a lot lower than the 11.5 percent Social Security tax), participants would have to average an annual real return of 10.7 percent in order to beat the current law Social Security benefit (Mitchell 1999, A-22). To do this with a 60-40 split between diversified stocks and bonds, you would need one heck of a good mutual fund. From 1926 through 1990, government bonds offered a 1.8 percent real annual yield, while the figure for stocks was 8.6 percent (Siegel 1992, 30–31). Recent government estimates (such as in U.S. General Accounting Office 1998, 39–40) predict that, in the future, bond yields may tend to be slightly higher and stock yields slightly lower. Barring something that is quite unanticipated, the weighted average of these yields is well below what it would take for an individual account to pay off.[3]

Archer and Shaw might almost just as well have said, therefore, that you would get your individual account at retirement only if, at that point, you were at least ten feet tall.[4] The main effect of their plan, therefore, would simply be to shovel money into the Trust Fund and reduce the reported budget surplus (while also perhaps directing business to Wall Street investment firms). Their Potemkin Village tax cuts and individual accounts were little more than ritualistic gestures.

The Archer-Shaw plan is unusual in proposing "individual accounts" that would have virtually no substance. However, it is not the only privatization plan in which individual accounts would have at least a partly sham character during the transition period by reason of an old-law benefit guarantee that is notionally funded by reducing what you get from your account. Martin Feldstein has proposed doing much the same thing as Archer and Shaw, except that retirees would get 25 percent of the accounts' value.

Feldstein illustrates his proposal as follows: Suppose that under current law your Social Security benefit would have been $1,300 per month, and that at retirement your individual account (funded by government contributions of 2.3 percent of your annual covered earnings) is large enough to fund an annuity of $800 per month. You get the current-law benefit ($1,300) plus one-quarter of the new-law annuity ($200), for a total of $1,500 per month, while the government takes the other $600 from your account and thus ostensibly reduces by that amount its cost of providing the current-law benefit (Feldstein 1999b, 42).[5] One could therefore describe the individual accounts here as being 75 percent a sham (just as under the Archer-Shaw plan) and 25 percent genuine.

Increasing National Saving through Full Funding

Turning from bookkeeping to the actual substance of privatization, proponents such as Martin Feldstein consider its most important feature to be increasing national saving through the shift to full funding. Suppose we assume that privatization actually would increase national saving, although this depends on how it is done. And suppose we ignore the fact that national saving could be increased by a variety of means outside as well as inside Social Security[6] and wholly without regard to privatization's other proposed changes. Is this policy change one that we should generally welcome?

Nearly all commentators who weigh in on the subject argue that we should save more. Yet whether they are right, rather than just parroting what their mothers taught them, is essentially a matter of taste plus soft empirical prediction. To save is to forego present consumption and thereby (one hopes) make possible increased future consumption. While a positive rate of return on saving indicates that we get better than a one-to-one return by trading present for future consumption, this is not by itself very informative.

Feldstein has stated that his argument for greater saving rests on two main factors: the "tax wedge" between the social and private return to investment, and the positive externality to future generations, who benefit from our saving but cannot transact with us to do more of it.[7] Yet the tax wedge cannot explain the entire claimed spread between a 9 percent real return and a 3 percent discount rate. And the externality problem may be offset if people who have some concern for the future tend to underestimate just how well-off future generations will be. One hundred years ago, who foresaw modern medicine, airplanes, computers, washing machines, and televisions? If the members of future generations will be sufficiently wealthier than us, then transferring consumption opportunities at the margin from ourselves to them may not be an attractive distributional policy from behind the veil unless the payoff is quite substantial.

Once we accept the existence of some doubt about the case for sharply increasing national saving, Feldstein's assumption for forecasting purposes that at the margin it earns a 9 percent return and should be discounted at only 3 percent begins to look shaky. His position on discounting is in any event hard to reconcile with conventional economic reasoning, which typically deduces preferences (such as those underlying discount rates) from behavior, and thus might suggest that nonsavers are optimizing as things stand. And on the positive return side, others argue that the economy-wide average real pretax return with risk is only about 6 percent (Bosworth 1996, 98), and that the return available at the margin if investment increases may not even be that great (Engen and Gale 1997). Thus, the claimed money machine from increasing national saving rests on an optimistic view of the returns that are available at the margin to extra saving, along with a rather extreme position about some combination of people's myopia, the level of tax distortion, and the needs of future compared to current generations.

Privatization and Portfolio Choice

When we turn to privatization's proposed effect on portfolio choice, it is useful to start by distinguishing two possible aims that may travel in tandem. The first is changing the Social Security portfolio that most or all people end up with, so that at least some of their life annuity benefits have a defined-contribution character and depend on the performance of a diverse asset portfolio containing stocks as well as bonds. The second aim is offering people more than one portfolio choice along various dimensions.

These two aims are related in a couple of respects. Increasing choice would result in portfolio changes for any participant who was dissatisfied with where current Social Security leaves him overall. And providing choice does not contradict deciding what many people will end up with, through the specification of a default choice that they often may fail to alter. Default choices are needed not only to determine the legal consequences of failing to elect, but also to reduce paperwork and provide guidance to people who are not sure what to do. The best default choice is that which prompts the least amount of filing to change it and/or offers the most beneficial package to people who are unlikely to file in any event. As it happens, Social Security reformers who favor broader portfolio choice also tend to favor a default choice that includes a stock-driven, defined-contribution component.

The attentive reader already knows that I am sympathetic on both counts to the privatizers. Although paternalism and moral hazard may support limiting portfolio choice, current Social Security's mandatory benefit package is hard to reconcile with any familiar theory of optimal choice by investors. Again, even the belief that people should be required to end up with life annuities and barred from making really foolish investment choices through the system falls short of supporting the single choice that is mandated today.

A good uniform or default choice might have more of a defined-contribution character than existing Social Security and would include stock ownership notwithstanding people's indirect stock market participation through the tax-transfer system. In addition, because people have varying risk preferences and may want to use Social Security in different ways as a component of their overall investment positions, we might want to offer them some choice within the system, even if it is relatively limited.

The range of investment choice that people might be allowed through

Social Security is infinitely variable, and need not be discussed in detail here. The possibilities range from "mandat[ing] the allocation of assets between stocks, bonds, and other investment categories during the accumulation phase and requir[ing] the purchase of a government annuity at retirement ... [to] allow[ing] substantial individual choice in the investment of assets and in the time profile and method of distributing accumulated assets" (Poterba and Wise 1998, 363).

We could, for example, allow people to choose only the percentages of their tax contributions that will go to different types of diversified asset baskets such as stocks and bonds. Or we might offer choice within a given asset type, such as by allowing investors to emphasize such categories as start-ups, technology stocks, international investment, or the Fortune 500. At the distribution end, the most prominent open issues include what if any continued investment risk to permit after retirement (such as through variable annuities with payoffs that depend on the stock market), and whether to offer a reduced annual payout in exchange for an inheritability feature.

Even those who agree about the desirability of changing and/or increasing portfolio choice within Social Security must acknowledge that it raises some real concerns. One is that if the government is deciding what stock investments by Social Security participants are permissible, the concerns about "Social Security socialism" that have mainly been debated with regard to direct government ownership of stocks may reemerge. To show this through exaggeration, suppose initially that in a nominally privatized Social Security system, people bought and held their own stocks through individual accounts, but the government told them exactly what stocks to hold at all times. Here the government's effective control over the allocation of Social Security stock investment, and more generally over corporate governance, would be the same as if it held the stock directly. In effect, Social Security participants would simply be its agents, executing its buy-sell commands.

As we gradually increase the range of permissible stock choice by investors, the government's allocative influence presumably declines. And if all we require is that any mutual fund meeting plain-vanilla business requirements can offer Social Security participants anything that meets some general diversification standard, then the government's ability to affect people's stock choices may be small indeed. (Of course, the same might be said about Trust Fund stock ownership that was mediated through mutual funds under the direction of an independent Social Security Reserve Board.)

Suppose, however, that Congress begins issuing legislative commands concerning stocks that either cannot or must be included in the portfolios that are offered to Social Security participants. Perhaps it would start by banning tobacco stocks, and then go on to require inclusion of Rust Belt manufacturers in key political swing states that are threatening to lay off workers. For better or worse, the allocative results of such interventions could be quite similar to those of having Congress dictate what stocks the Trust Fund should hold. Perhaps the main difference between the two cases is simply the possibility that the proponents of these interventions would have a tougher sell politically if the effect on returns of choosing stocks on noneconomic grounds showed up directly in voters' individual accounts, rather than via a collective Trust Fund that was notionally underwriting a defined-benefit plan.

A second big concern about changing and increasing portfolio choice under Social Security goes to its likely effect on the system's administrative costs. The current system's low annual administrative cost reflects that almost all it does is collect taxes (a function that piggybacks on income tax compliance), issue benefit checks, and track the use of government bonds to hold its deemed positive cash flow. Providing more complex and diverse choices to participants is unavoidably costlier. Peter Diamond estimates that even a relatively low-cost, low-service alternative of the sort privatizers contemplate would cost about $40 to $50 per worker per year (1999, 2), and that this, for workers whose covered earnings were at the mean, would be equivalent to a onetime 9 to 11 percent charge on all new contributions to the system (10). Others suggest that costs could be held to the $31 to $39 range for the average account if passively managed and providing only limited customer services (James et al. 1999, 31), but this is still an increase compared to the costs of the current system.

Here a privatizer might offer such replies as the following: You get what you pay for; choice and service are worth paying for; most of us don't keep money in our mattresses despite the transactional cost savings; and surely few would advocate having the government economize on the costs of consumer choice and competitive marketing by "impos[ing] one-size-fits-all in . . . markets such as automobiles, breakfast cereal, or personal computers" (Mulligan and Sala-i-Martin 1999c, 22). Still, the existence of a tradeoff is hard to deny, especially for small accounts and for people who like the choice that is currently offered.

One way to address the administrative cost problem is to make the default choice as basic, no frills, and low cost as possible, while permitting people to choose higher and costlier service levels on the view that they will only do so when they consider the benefit worth the cost (Goldberg and

Graetz 1999). Financial planning is, however, an area where many observers think there tends to be a lot of wasted effort. Many mutual funds and people acting on their own account arguably trade too much if the objective is to make as much money as possible for the investor, not just to generate broker-age fees or have fun spinning the roulette wheel. And the *Wall Street Journal* regularly reports on the touted fund managers who are unable to outperform its interns who literally picked stocks by throwing darts at the wall. Thus, pa-ternalistic arguments could reasonably extend to limiting the costly service options that a privatized Social Security system makes available.

Administrative Privatization

A decision to broaden or at least alter portfolio choice within Social Security would give new impetus to the question of whether competing private firms should participate in its operations. In particular, the firms could hold and in-vest people's individual account balances and perhaps manage benefit dis-bursement. This, at last, is a proposal for which the word "privatization" seems entirely apt.

This administrative issue is linked to that of portfolio choice because of the relative organizational advantages of competitive private suppliers as compared to bureaucrats. For simple and well-defined tasks where econ-omies of scale matter and performance is easy to measure, bureaucracies of-ten perform quite well (Wilson 1991). Traditional Social Security is limited to such tasks and performs them with "remarkable precision" (35), but pri-vate firms might be much better at catering to a wide range of investor pref-erences. Whether the issue is one of suitable relative pricing of alternative benefit packages, attentive customer service, or innovation in benefit pack-ages, the classic private versus public distinction that several decades of American versus Soviet shoe manufacture made obvious is right on point if—but it is a big if—we consider this a standard consumer market.

Take, for example, the question of what to think about the advertising costs that competitive private firms would presumably incur and pass on to customers if they were involved in administering people's Social Security ac-counts. Advocates of traditional Social Security regard this as pure waste, and even if privatization is adopted, they are sympathetic to barring the firms from "attempting to influence investors' choices through aggressive selling or advertising" (Aaron and Reischauer 1998, 87). In free markets, however, advertising can be a tool for giving consumers greater information and choice. Thus, in the cigarette industry, the major producers are said to be de-lighted that the ban on television advertising helps keep new rivals and products (potentially including less deadly ones) from emerging, and thereby protects their cozy cartel. If we are sufficiently sanguine about consumers' exercise of portfolio choice in Social Security, advertising should be viewed in the main as a service tool, not a cost.

For several reasons, however, this consumer market might be considered too poorly functioning for the classic advantages of competitive activity to apply, at least in full. Suppose you start from the premise that a lot of financial planning activity has pretty thin benefits to begin with, at least if we take its aim to be maximizing earnings rather than having fun through an alternative to playing the horses. Then consider the massive number of small individual accounts that a privatized Social Security system would involve—perhaps as many as 150 million in all (Diamond 1999, 3). Add in the fact that, in 1996, two-thirds of all workers had covered earnings below $25,000 (Goldberg and Graetz 1999, 5), thus suggesting that the amount at stake in many cases would be pretty low. Finally, consider the level of knowledge and perhaps interest in financial planning matters that we observe in a society where half the public apparently does not know the difference between a stock and a bond (Diamond 1999, 8). Under these circumstances, one cannot too readily dismiss the view that "consumer lethargy" is too great here for competitive markets, or even the offering of greater rather than lesser choice, to have their usual advantages (20).[8] Thus, even the use of private firms might be accompanied by limiting the participants (for example, through a bidding process) and following the lead of some other countries by adopting measures to discourage aggressive marketing (James et al. 1999, 24–26).

To be sure, giving people individual accounts might induce them to become better informed. However, small stakes would induce only small efforts. And if you happen to support forced saving and limited portfolio choice through Social Security because you are skeptical about many people's long-term planning abilities, you may be inclined toward pessimism here even if you expect significant effort.

Accordingly, the administrative question of whether competitive private firms should be brought in to offer investment services to Social Security participants is closely linked to the stance you take concerning the proper level of portfolio choice. No one could seriously think that the Social Security Administration is well suited to offer more than a very limited menu of plain-vanilla investment choices. And it is hard to argue against, at the least, offering cheap "no-frills" options that, even if privately administered, would set both cost and service at low levels. Whether to offer higher-cost, higher-service options as well, necessarily administered by private firms, depends on the view you take of consumer choice in this market.

Eliminating Social Security's Transfer Content

The final important proposed change in the privatization bundle is eliminating Social Security's transfer content. While the current system aims at progressivity via the interaction of a flat-rate tax on covered earnings with a declining-rate benefit formula, privatizers generally envision having people's tax contributions go straight into their own individual accounts without any transfer through the system from high earners to low earners. The idea is to eliminate the various net wage taxes and subsidies that may distort people's labor market decisions under the current system (Feldstein 1998, 4–8).

This idea is open to criticism on a couple of grounds. One is that the social cost of discouraging work effort needs to be traded off against the benefit of offering social insurance protection with respect to earning ability. If you support the use of any work-conditioned tax base, such as income or consumption, to allocate tax burdens, then—be you a flat-taxer or a believer in steeply graduated income tax rates—you apparently favor discouraging work effort to some extent for distributional reasons. We thus are just haggling over the price.

Suppose for the moment that the rest of the tax-transfer system is fixed and cannot be adjusted to compensate for the elimination of progressive transfers through Social Security. Only if the rest of the system is sufficiently progressive should simply eliminating Social Security's redistributive content be considered unobjectionable. People may disagree about this, but surely it requires more discussion than it has been getting from privatizers.

A second problem with eliminating Social Security's net wage taxes and subsidies is that in some cases it might not even reduce labor market distortion. In our society, by far the highest marginal tax rates are borne by certain relatively poor households—those with children that are at or slightly above the poverty line. On every extra dollar that these households earn, they not only pay various taxes, but may bear a reduction (or in some cases abrupt elimination) of various income-conditioned transfers, such as those under Temporary Assistance to Needy Families, Food Stamps, Medicaid, and certain federal housing programs. I have elsewhere estimated that, in some plausible worst-case scenarios, a one-parent, two-child household may be financially better off earning $10,000 a year than $25,000 (Shaviro 1999).

Due to variations between transfer programs and their implementation in different states, it would be hard to use a uniform nationwide Social Security system as a well-focused tool to offset the particular cases where poor and near-poor households face wildly excessive marginal tax rates. The better course would be to rationalize and better integrate those programs. Nonetheless, for lower-income households that face very high marginal tax rates on balance, zeroing out Social Security's transfer content should not necessarily fly under the banner of reducing labor market distortion.

If you favor greater progressive redistribution than the tax-transfer system currently accomplishes independently of Social Security, why not accept privatizers' position on this and simply shift the transfer content to some other set of programs? There are two possible arguments for wanting to continue not just current progressivity, but Social Security's contribution to it. The first is that, as a political matter, this contribution cannot readily be shifted to, say, the income tax and welfare systems. This could be a claim about short-term political rigidities if Social Security reform would be killed by linking it to a broader menu of controversial changes. Or it could be a claim about the long-term political equilibrium if traditionalists are right that intermingling Social Security's transfer content with its forced saving content increases a befuddled public's tolerance for progressive redistribution.

The second possible argument for continuing to use Social Security in this way goes to its possible technical advantages as a redistributive tool—for example, because it pays age-conditioned benefits and can use information about lifetime, not just annual, earnings. Here once again, privatization and the current system should not be thought of as polar alternatives that exhaust all of the possibilities.

Spousal and Household Issues in Privatization

One set of important Social Security issues that as yet have received little attention in the emerging privatization debate are those concerning spousal benefits. Privatization studies often assume the continuation of present law spousal benefits (Feldstein and Ranguelova 1999, 22 n. 20), whether due to a broader (and perhaps misguided) commitment to grandfathering all present-law benefits or because one can only tackle so many issues at the same time. Obviously, however, there is considerable tension between the transfer content of the existing spousal rules and many privatizers' hostility to transfers through Social Security (and perhaps more generally).

In principle, privatization could be further adapted to accommodate the retirement needs of households with two retirees. Feldstein and Ranguelova mention the possibility of providing double life annuities, under which a given retiree's benefits would continue until the death of both the retiree and his spouse (1999, 22). We could modify this idea to have the benefit decline by a specified percentage when one spouse dies, thus permitting more of the actuarial value of the retirement package to be allocated to the period when both spouses are alive and needs are therefore greater. In addition, we could provide the equivalent of earnings-sharing by giving each spouse equal rights with respect to retirement account contributions and returns generated during a marriage. Or at least the accounts could be made expressly divisible between the spouses in divorce settlements.

The fact that a household with two adults but only one worker may need greater forced saving for retirement than a household with just one adult would in theory be easy to address in a privatized system, by requiring extra tax contributions that would purchase extra benefits. While perhaps politically inconvenient, privatization's strengthened tax-benefit link might at least make it less of an uphill climb politically than similar proposals under the current Social Security system. Any transfer consequences of having two adults rather than one in a household presumably would have to be handled through the income tax, welfare system, and the like.

Summary

"Privatizing" Social Security is quite different than privatizing the post office or a government-run national health care system. As used in the debate over Social Security reform, the term is somewhat of a misnomer for a bundle of proposals that would do a lot more than just turn over certain operations to private firms. In particular, "privatization" involves a shift to full funding that proponents hope will increase national saving, the offering of greater portfolio choice within Social Security, and elimination of the system's transfer content. It also is associated with a bookkeeping shift to "individual accounts" and with the claim that increasing national saving provides a kind of money machine that earns a 9 percent return and costs only 3 percent. All of these elements in the privatization package can, and for purposes of clear thinking should, be analyzed separately.

My own thumbnail responses to these various proposals are as follows:
• Increasing national saving is a plausible although not overwhelmingly persuasive aim. However, privatizers often overstate the link between this aim and the level of advance funding of Social Security. National saving can be increased by a variety of means without addressing Social Security, and it is possible that a funding increase would do little to affect national saving.

- "Individual accounts" is not a well-defined term. One could say they exist today, since the Social Security Administration keeps track of tax and earnings data on an individualized basis, and given the widespread belief that accruing benefits are to some extent a vested entitlement. A bookkeeping shift to keeping track of Social Security funds more on an individualized basis, and less through the collective accounting entries represented by the Social Security Trust Fund, might conceivably discourage the enactment of tax cuts and spending increases. The mechanism, however, would be the same as that of reducing the reported budget surplus through errors in budget arithmetic.

- Standard views of optimal investment strategy provide some support both for changing the basic or default package that Social Security offers to have more of a defined-contribution character (with diversified stocks playing a role) and for giving participants some choice between investment strategies and benefit packages. But the value of choice depends on how attentively and well you think people will exercise it. Moreover, providing bounded choice with respect to stocks may revive concern about government intervention to affect the allocation of investment between companies through the Social Security system. And the transaction costs of offering greater choice may give you pause even if you normally consider them well worth the benefit of letting consumers get what they want.

- Administrative privatization is valuable and indeed verging on necessary if Social Security is modified to offer a great deal of portfolio choice. However, it may be needlessly costly if the new system offers only limited choice and/or we conclude that participants cannot do a good job of evaluating competing sales pitches from private firms.

- Privatizers have offered little explanation for eliminating Social Security's transfer content. Using an otherwise "privatized" Social Security system to transfer wealth from high earners to low earners might increase labor market distortion (depending on interactions with the rest of the tax-transfer system), but you might as well support a uniform head tax if you are wholly unwilling to contemplate such distortions in exchange for social insurance benefits. Social Security's transfer content should depend both on how it will affect overall redistribution (relative to what we conclude is best) and on the general suitability of retirement pensions as a redistributive tool.

8 A Modest Proposal: Progressive Privatization

Service with a Smile

In P. G. Wodehouse's classic stories about the feckless London boulevardier Bertie Wooster and his infallible "gentleman's personal gentleman" Jeeves, there is a time when Jeeves decides that the two of them will go on a round-the-world boat cruise. Bertie, who likes to thinks he is the master, resists. When Jeeves keeps showing him travel brochures from the cruise ship companies, Bertie observes: "His whole attitude recalled irresistibly to the mind that of some assiduous hound who will persist in laying a dead rat on the drawing room carpet, though repeatedly apprised by word and gesture that the market for same is sluggish or even nonexistent" (Wodehouse 1975 ed., 8). But Jeeves naturally prevails in the end, leaving Bertie to bleat: "Perhaps that cruise won't be so very foul after all?" (222) before Jeeves reveals that he has purchased the tickets without even waiting for Bertie's say-so.

Any author of a book on a hot topic of current policy debate is in a sense a would-be Jeeves, if only in his own fevered fantasy. The relationship to the reader, who presumably seeks information or amusement, is no less one of service than providing a shoeshine. Yet the Jeevesian temptation to lead and guide, not just serve, is always there and may indeed be the task's chief compensation. While no mortal writer can match the paragon Jeeves and few readers are as tractable as Bertie Wooster, both parties should keep in mind the dynamics of a car dealership, where when the salesman asks, "Can I help you?" he also means, "Can I get you to help me?" The main difference here is just that "help" may be a matter of psychic or ideological rather than monetary gratification.

Is everything so far in this book therefore just the windup to a pitch—my own pet Social Security reform proposal? Well, as it happens . . . yes and no.

Many of the choices posed by Social Security reform do not have obviously dominant solutions and in the end must turn on contestable personal values and empirical hunches. That is one reason why I have mainly sought just to illuminate the underlying choices that we face, albeit without declining to express opinions where they seemed warranted. Yet these opinions actually imply a very general approach to Social Security reform, although with lots of the details left open, that (here comes the sales pitch) is superior in key respects to both traditionalist Social Security reform and privatization. Since this approach follows organically from the book's analysis, I begin by reviewing the main points that the prior seven chapters have made.

Main Conclusions concerning Social Security Reform
Clear Thinking versus Clown Family Accounting

Social Security is just a part of a larger tax-transfer system that matters solely insofar as it affects people. "Saving Social Security" is therefore not a project akin to saving the whales. The goal of Social Security reform should be to optimize the allocative and distributional effects of our overall fiscal system, given the applicable economic and political constraints on what we can do. Arithmetic exercises in how one change or another would affect the system's projected long-term solvency therefore fall considerably short of adequately addressing the issues. If the arithmetic pertaining to an arbitrary subset of overall government fiscal transactions were all that mattered, we could restore Social Security's projected long-term solvency by not charging benefit payouts against the Trust Fund whenever an officially designated little child yelled, "1-2-3–Red light!" just before they were mailed.

A Tax and a Subsidy That Are Not Well Correlated

Social Security consists of a wage tax plus a wage subsidy, with the former being payable while you work and the latter being provided when you retire. The result for any given worker is a net wage tax or a net wage subsidy, depending on which has greater value on a lifetime basis. Social Security's combination of a flat-rate tax on covered earnings with a declining-rate benefit formula aids low earners relative to high earners. However, overall progressivity relative to earnings is considerably reduced by the benefit formula's ignoring life expectancy, which generally is greater for high earners.

One problem with the current package is that the unclarity of the relationship between earning an extra dollar today and receiving greater Social Security benefits may induce people to err in the direction of overestimating the extent to which the system actually penalizes decisions to work and earn more. A second problem is that the separate-track computation of taxes and benefits impedes giving the system a coherent or consistent transfer content.

For example, differences in annual wage path may cause two people with equivalent lifetime earnings to fare unequally under the system. And the fact that Social Security taxes are levied purely on an individual basis while benefits depend on marital status leads to what are probably excessive transfers to single-earner couples (with the most affluent such households getting the largest household-related transfers) and excessive discouragement of market work by secondary-earner spouses.

While specific problems of this kind can always be addressed by tinkering with the tax and benefit formulas, the current Social Security system more or less invites them to occur by running the tax and benefit computations on separate tracks. The most plausible purpose that the separate tracks serve is to permit wise and virtuous experts, if people of this description happen to have just the right intermediate quantum of political power, to impose by obfuscation good policies that they cannot impose straightforwardly. But it is hard to be confident that obscuring the system's transfer content has good effects on balance.

Social Security's Three Main Components

The Social Security benefits (B) that any participant receives can tautologically be described through the equation $B = T + rT + X$, where T equals Social Security taxes paid, rT equals the investment return attributed to these taxes, and X is the positive or negative transfer needed to equalize the left- and right-hand sides of the equation. What makes this exercise useful, rather than whimsical, is its distinguishing the system's three main functions: inducing forced retirement saving by participants (albeit without any necessary effect on national saving), denying portfolio choice with respect to the forced saving, and transferring lifetime wealth between participants. The first two of these functions can in principle be reversed by participants through transactions outside the system, such as dissaving and adjusting the rest of their investment portfolios, but nonetheless are probably significant in practice for most Americans. The justification, if any, for these three functions of Social Security lies in the broad realm of the government's role in providing social insurance.

Social Security and Social Insurance

The aim of insurance could be described as providing money in states of the world where you will value it more rather than less. Social insurance, provided mandatorily by the government, is most likely to be a good idea where market failures such as adverse selection impede its being offered cost-effectively by private firms. In practice, social insurance should mainly deal with problems of comprehensive income risk, because people presumably care about their overall circumstances while private insurance is best suited to deal with isolated transactions.

Risk-spreading, the classic technique of private insurance, may be suitably combined with risk prevention (akin to speed limits and seat belt laws) when social insurance is in the picture. From this perspective, paternalism and problems of moral hazard may plausibly be invoked to support Social Security's inducing forced saving and barring foolish or overly risky portfolio choice with regard to this saving. As for Social Security's transfer content, which at its best is progressive with an age component, this is an area of substantial overlap with income and other taxes as well as various income-conditioned transfer programs. However, Social Security may have a role to play here either as a matter of optimal program design or by reason of short- or long-term political constraints on how progressive redistribution can be accomplished.

The Economics of System Funding

The degree of advance funding of a private retirement plan, such as an employer's pension fund for employees, matters because a contractually binding set-aside of adequate funds greatly mitigates the danger that the employer will renege or default. These considerations have less application to Social Security, since the government is unlikely to face involuntary default, has no incentive to renege if retirees are politically powerful, and if it does want to renege cannot be stopped from doing so through a mechanism far short of creating binding debt obligations (and perhaps not even by that). Thus, apart from any Cowardly Lion effect, whereby bookkeeping affects political decisions because people think it is meaningful, the only economic significance of Social Security funding relates to the effects that the aggregate tax-benefit relationship over time may have on national saving.

Historically, Social Security's lack of full funding has reduced national saving through an income effect on members of older age cohorts, who have received benefits that younger age cohorts pay for, and thus can spend more on consumption during their working and retirement years. This income effect is regrettable if you happen to favor increased national saving. Even if you do, however, the progressivity of the intergenerational transfer from younger to older generations should be kept in mind as well.

The Politics of Social Security Trust Fund Accounting

The Social Security Trust Fund is an artifact of whatever bookkeeping rules Congress happens to prescribe, and thus bears only a rough relationship to questions of the long-term funding relationship between Social Security taxes and benefit payments. As such, it matters only insofar as people think that it matters (or as a legal trigger device, since its formal exhaustion would require congressional action to keep benefit checks flowing). The view that Social Security ought to be self-financing has historically constrained allowable Trust Fund bookkeeping. However, the constraint is now at risk due to the mania for "saving Social Security" by notionally "investing" a portion of the budget surplus in the Trust Fund. The supposed "investment" may have short-term political virtues if, by reducing the reported budget surplus, it dissuades Congress from enacting tax cuts or spending increases that happen to be bad policy. It has a long-term vice, however, in that it weakens a political limitation on retirees' capacity to demand a larger share of the pie. Social Security's self-financing norm was originally adopted to ensure that retirement benefits would not be unduly cut, but its main value today, given retirees' vast political power, lies in any capacity it might have to discourage undue benefit expansion. This capacity is at risk if politicians find that they can increase the Trust Fund whenever they like without actually having to impose the visible burden of a forthrightly announced payroll tax increase.

The Problems with Traditionalist Social Security Reform

Traditionalists rightly point out that the system's financing problems in no way necessitate changing its basic structure. The current system is sufficiently flexible (or to put it less charitably, lacking in well-defined policy content) to permit any number of tax and benefit changes that would restore its long-term projected solvency, even if we forego all bookkeeping games. And for anyone who actually cares about the policy content of these changes, the sheer range ensures that some are bound to have some appeal. For example, if you value progressivity, you may prefer fuller income taxation of benefits to methods of cutting benefits that have more of an across-the-board effect—say, a retirement age increase or inclusion of additional years in average indexed monthly earnings (AIME).

Yet the traditionalists' attachment to the present system, however understandable as a product of one's personal or our national history, should not get in the way of a cold-eyed assessment of the system's structural defects. These are, in particular, the arguable concealment of its wage subsidy, Rube Goldberg transfer machinery, and offering only one (perhaps unduly conservative) portfolio choice. Such features should invite rethinking the system's structure even if the long-term financing picture substantially improves.

The main area in which traditionalists have advocated Social Security reform on fundamental, not just financing, grounds is that of spousal benefits. Some prominent suggestions, such as capping the spousal benefit or perhaps imposing earnings-sharing (the clearest advantages of which relate to the treatment of divorce), might indeed improve the system. But proper treatment of married versus single households requires focusing on the distinction between (a) extra forced saving by and (b) extra transfers to married households in which only one spouse worked. While the current system provides the latter, the case for the former is stronger. The existing system could in theory be revised in this direction—for example, by requiring one-earner couples to pay for their extra benefits through extra Social Security taxes that might be collected via income tax returns. But its lack of a clear tax-benefit link may discourage thinking in these terms.

The Problems with Privatization

If portfolio choice is as good for our political system as for rational investors, then it is a shame that one bundled set of proposed changes, going by the name of privatization, has so dominated public discussion of significant reform. Privatizers raise many of the right issues but are not, as the term seems to imply, mainly suggesting that we harness market forces to improve the goods and services that are offered to consumers. Rather, they propose multiple independent changes, the most important of which are (a) increasing system funding in the hope of increasing national saving, (b) shifting from what is mainly a defined-benefit plan with no portfolio choice by participants to a defined-contribution plan that offers some choice and perhaps encourages well-diversified stock market investment, and (c) eliminating transfers within the system, other than those that result from guaranteeing current-law benefits.

Privatizers' aim of increasing national saving through greater Social Security funding raises questions about whether the advantages of thus swapping some present for future consumption are great enough to warrant the burden on current workers, who may be less wealthy on a lifetime basis than future workers. The proposals to increase portfolio choice and bring in private firms on the administrative end are potentially appealing but require hard thinking about just how much choice is best for small accounts that are owned by possibly ill-informed consumers who may have good reason (given the amounts at stake) to remain ill-informed and largely passive. And the privatizers' opposition to progressive redistribution through Social Security is not self-evidently correct even if the current system is not all that progressive given its treatment of life expectancy.

A Modest Proposal at Last

Ambrose Bierce defined a critic as one who "boasts himself hard to please because nobody tries to please him" (1993 ed., 20). An even less charitable view might hold that the critic is to the active proponent like the draft dodger to the soldier, or perhaps the flea to the dog. Lest that be so, herewith a brief sketch of my own proposed approach to Social Security reform.

I start with the view that a tax-transfer system, considered without regard to the labels that we attach to particular parts, should (a) tax work for distributional reasons, but to an extent that is constrained by concern about the resulting inefficient deterrence of work; (b) provide income support to people in sufficient need, subject to whatever limitations are thought necessary as "tough love" to induce suitable work effort; and (c) require some minimum level of retirement saving that the saver cannot invest too foolishly or riskily.

A system that we call "Social Security" will indubitably perform the third of these functions and may contribute to the first two as well. I would propose to continue the use of Social Security in progressive redistribution for political convenience and due to its use of lifetime earnings information, along with the case for providing a bit of extra poverty relief to the elderly compared to those of working age.

For want of a better name, I call my proposal "progressive privatization," although it does not include measures designed to increase national saving—the core feature in privatization according to Martin Feldstein. Perhaps the easiest way to increase national saving is by transferring wealth from low to high marginal savers—for example, from current to future generations. While this transfer can be accomplished through Social Security, such as by raising the tax or cutting benefits while holding constant the path of other taxes and government spending, the question of whether to do this has little natural connection to the other design issues raised by Social Security reform.

Under my proposal, once the reform process had been completed, the Social Security system would have the following features:

Mandatory Contributions

Earnings up to some ceiling would be withheld from workers (it's fair in isolation to call this a "tax") and deposited in the workers' "individual accounts."

As a matter of practicality, the ceiling might need to be applied on a purely annual basis, as under present Social Security law. The use of a ceiling would reflect the view that forced saving need not increase indefinitely with earnings. The individual account label would reflect a strengthened and more transparent tax-benefit link, as well as facilitating the exercise of portfolio choice and perhaps discouraging Congress from treating positive cash flows to the system as a goad to the enactment of tax cuts or spending increases that were otherwise undesirable.

Extra Contributions by One-Earner Couples

For married couples (and other true couples that could be identified and Congress could be persuaded to recognize), tax contributions by either spouse would be split 50-50 between the two spouses' individual accounts. The overall tax contribution required from a couple would be greater than that required from a single individual with the same earnings. In cases where both spouses had significant earnings and at least one earned more than the ceiling, this would happen automatically through Social Security tax withholding at the workplace. Where only one spouse had significant earnings, the extra tax contribution would presumably have to be collected via income tax returns.

Portfolio Choice While Working

Individual accounts would be invested in diversified assets including stocks and bonds, passively managed with some involvement of private firms but significant limits on consumer choice and permissible marketing. Exactly how best to resolve the tradeoff between expanding choice (which may also reduce risks of political interference in investment allocation) and reducing administrative cost is a subject on which I confess to lacking precise views.

Progressive Redistribution

The system would include a progressivity adjustment to aid low earners relative to high earners. To explore how this could be done, let's start with a relatively straightforward method and then consider alternatives that might have political or administrative advantages. Suppose initially that we had full information when people retired about their lifetime earnings (not limited to the annual ceiling), at the least from working and perhaps from investment outcomes as well. We could then, at the moment of retirement, mandate a onetime progressive transfer from the accounts of people who were high earners on a lifetime basis to those who were low earners. The amount in your individual account after the (positive or negative) progressivity transfer had been made would then determine the value of the retirement benefits that you could purchase with it.

One problem with this approach is that it might unduly reward deliberate decisions not to work (such as through early retirement, extra years of schooling, or staying home to raise children) that presumably did not make you worse off. In response, the progressivity adjustment might be based on average annual, rather than lifetime, earnings, with years of such nonwork being excluded from the denominator used in computing in the average. As always in distributional policy, we would have to determine the relevance of household status. The fact that your spouse has a high individual account balance or high career earnings may be relevant to the transfer that we decide you should make or receive.

One problem with this pure form of the progressivity adjustment is that it requires information about people's lifetime earnings that might not be readily available. So, at the cost of accuracy in implementing distribution policy, the relevant distributional information could be limited to people's covered earnings (those subject to the mandatory contribution). It could depend as well on the investment performance of their individual accounts. Under this approach, the transfer might depend purely on account balances at retirement, which would be adjusted through the application of a positive and negative tax rate schedule.

In illustration, suppose there was a rule barring overall transfers to or from the group of individual accounts belonging to all the people who retired in a given year. (Such a rule might conceivably provide a useful political constraint, but I suggest it here just to simplify the exposition.) One way of making the progressivity adjustment—although the arithmetic possibilities are infinite—would be to make no adjustment to accounts that were exactly at the average for the year, while applying, say, a 30 percent positive and negative tax rate to departures from the average. Thus, if the average account size for a year was $200,000, then an account that stood at zero would be increased to $60,000, while one that stood at $100,000 would be increased to $130,000, and one that stood at $1 million would be reduced to $760,000. Obviously, marginal rates could be either higher or lower than this, and graduated rather than flat. Moreover, the zero-adjustment point could be higher or lower than the year's average even assuming an annual break-even requirement.

While administratively feasible, this approach could be criticized as engendering too much uncertainty about how much of your account the government will end up letting you keep, given the difficulty of credible pre-commitment concerning future political decisions. But a variety of other means could be used to approximate the result.

For example, taxes on and transfers to individual accounts could be provided annually during the contribution period, thus sacrificing the lifetime perspective but perhaps facilitating the use of non–Social Security income and earnings information from the same year. (President Clinton's 1999 proposal to establish "USA accounts" outside Social Security suggested something like this, by having the government contribute to people's retirement accounts subject to an income phaseout.) Or the special taxes and transfers could be imposed on annual distributions during the retirement period. Or the job of making distributional adjustments could be left to the income tax, through its rules for the taxation of contributions when made and distributions when received.

Portfolio Choice upon Retirement

Upon retirement, a second-stage portfolio choice issue arises concerning permissible benefit packages. Presumably, a life annuity (and for couples, perhaps a double life annuity) should be at least a major part of the package. At least some portion of this life annuity should be fixed in real terms. Amounts in excess of this, however, could take the form of a variable annuity in which, say, the performance of the stock market might influence what benefits were paid each year. This design is familiar to pension professionals, who would call this a "floor plan"—a defined-contribution plan with a defined-benefit minimum or floor level (Bodie 1999, 8)—but the details are beyond my present scope.

Under the method I described above for one-time progressivity adjustments to individual account balances upon retirement, every American would get at least something toward the prevention of destitution in his retirement years, since accounts that stood at zero would be adjusted upward. This approximates the creation of a fixed annual "demogrant" for the elderly through Social Security.

Bequest Alternatives

To improve the tax-benefit link, improve and/or increase portfolio choice, and address the distributional effects on Social Security of systematic differences in life expectancy, various bequest alternatives could be offered. For example, people who died before retirement could be empowered to leave their individual accounts (net of any progressivity adjustments) to spouses, children, or anyone else they chose. In addition, those who died shortly after retirement could be permitted to make bequests given how little they had gotten out of the system. An example would be a "ten-year-certain life annuity," under which payments for that period are guaranteed, and thus go to the heirs if the retiree dies early (Feldstein and Ranguelova 1999, 19). Either pre- or post-retirement bequest options could be made elective on an actuarially fair basis, by having the account holders pay for them through otherwise lower benefits.

The "Transition Path" Problem, or, Getting There from Here

The above scheme is meant to do no more than lay a very general groundwork for discussion among those who are sympathetic to this book's analysis or who simply favor having more Social Security reform options on the table. So long as the heavens remain silent concerning the prospects for this scheme's adoption, further fleshing it out may not be practical enough to be practical, or interesting enough to be interesting. I also personally lack strong views concerning some of the important tradeoffs. This is where writers of hopeful temperament like to deploy the phrase "directions for future research."

One problem that is hard to ignore altogether, however, is the so-called "transition path" problem of how to get there from here given the existence of vast benefit promises under existing Social Security that are partly unfunded and partly expected to be funded through present-law payroll tax collections. While this, too, is not a problem that need be solved here and now, questions of basic feasibility and how to approach the change of systems will naturally occur to the thoughtful reader.

Since the new system, with its defined-contribution character, would pay for itself so long as the positive and negative transfers between individual accounts were in balance, the problem is simply one of financing old-law benefits that are not eliminated. On a number of grounds, the old-law benefits should not be considered entirely guaranteed. They were more or less self-awarded by older age cohorts without full financing in a political process where the ultimate payors were not represented. Not all of the prospective recipients are especially needy. One of the main incentive effects of eliminating some benefits might be to induce people to save more on their own if government retirement promises are not entirely trustworthy—possibly a good thing if you favor increased national saving. And the political power of the elderly creates grounds for hope that Social Security benefits will not over time be excessively curtailed. (For a fuller analysis of these points, see

Shaviro 2000, chapter 10.) Finally, even if you consider the existing benefit rules an implicit promise that the government ought to keep, you are interpreting current policy rather selectively if you ignore that the benefits are not fully financed (contrary to the system's core self-financing principle). In a very real sense, to guarantee the existing system's uncertain and underfunded benefits is to increase them, not just preserve them, without clear justification.

Reduction of existing benefits on some distributionally suitable basis therefore ought not to be ruled out as part of the solution to the financing problem. (And in any event it would be Clown family accounting to say that benefits must be protected but the people whose benefits are protected may be taxed to pay for them.) For the rest, we simply face a standard distributional question concerning the allocation of fiscal burdens, just as we would if an expensive war had to be paid for somehow. This question is important, but not as distinctive to Social Security (and thus able to be illuminated by this book's analysis) as the question of what the new system should look like.

A Final Word on Social Security Reform

The writer W. W. Jacobs (1998 ed.) tells the story of a magical monkey's paw that grants three wishes to its owner. An older couple gets it one day and wishes for two hundred pounds. The wish is promptly granted through a horrid machine accident that kills their beloved son, for which his employer offers them two hundred pounds' compensation. Their second wish is to get him back. So out of the grave he comes, as mangled as at the moment he died, to pound ominously on their door. Wish 3 is for a restoration of the state of affairs prevailing before they found the monkey's paw. This is granted with no tricks.

Americans of all ideological stripes are anxious for government action to "save Social Security." Some want to "privatize" the system or else to "invest" the surplus in the Trust Fund or the Trust Fund in the stock market. But what we wish for must be thought through carefully lest we get it, even though no force so diabolical as the monkey's paw is waiting to exploit the smallest underspecification. Effects on people are what matter, not effects on an artificially defined system, and the effects that matter depend on overall substance, not just line-drawing or labels or bookkeeping. A debate about the real substance of our distribution and retirement policies would at the least be more edifying than the battle of clichés that often passes in our society for political deliberation. And a clear-eyed focus on the underlying substance might even—who knows?—lead in the end to a better system.

Notes

Chapter One

1. Two further functions of Social Security could perhaps be teased out. The first is providing financial protection to members of a worker's family through rules, described in chapter 2, that provide certain spousal and survivorship benefits. The second, closely related to portfolio choice, is providing a kind of financial instrument that some analysts have argued might otherwise be unavailable to savers: a life annuity with a fixed real payment and Social Security's particular spousal and survivorship attributes.

Chapter Two

1. Additional rules ensure that self-employed individuals will basically come out with the same tax liability as a separate employer and worker considered in unison.

2. For example, suppose I earn $10,000 that is subject to the payroll tax but to no other taxes or withholding. The employer and I each nominally pay $765 to the government. The employer thus pays out a total of $10,765, while I receive $9,235. To say that I bear the entire tax is to say that I would otherwise have received the full $10,765. Thus, the tax I have really borne is $1,530 out of $10,765, or approximately 14.2 percent. In addition, adjusting for the exclusion of the employer share, the annual ceiling on wages that are subject to Social Security tax is actually about $78,150 (for 1999), not $72,600.

3. The effective rate of Social Security tax is complicated by interactions with other taxes at various levels of government. For example, under the federal income tax, an employer typically can deduct the entire payroll tax if incurred in the business setting, while a worker must include in taxable income his but not the employer's nominal share of the tax liability.

4. Wage indexing ensures that earlier years' earnings will not look lower than later ones just because wages generally or price levels were lower at the time.

5. A counterargument in favor of using dropout years might be that, without them, relative benefits would be unduly cut for women whose working careers were shortened by their acceptance of primary responsibility in the raising of their children. Yet the real point this problem makes is not that a subset of career earnings is generally more informative than overall career earnings, but rather that Social Security (like tax and transfer programs generally) raises important gender issues that require comprehensive atten-

tion. Given these issues' complexity, this book, alas, cannot be the place in which such attention is provided.

6. The dollar amounts in the rate brackets depend on your year of birth so they can be indexed to wage growth (which prevents the first two brackets from gradually disappearing over time). For workers who were born in 1937 and thus will reach age 65 in 2002, the 90 percent reimbursement rate applies to annualized AIME from 0 to $6,060, the 32 percent rate from $6,060 to $36,516, and the 15 percent rate above $36,516.

7. On the other hand, a lower discount rate also reduces the measured significance of the advantage higher earners garner from living longer on average.

8. Driving older workers out of the workforce may benefit younger workers but is unlikely to reduce unemployment in the long run (Miron and Weil 1997, 18). The possible benefit to younger workers of driving out their competition is hard to make into a principled argument for the Social Security earnings test. Any supplier in a market can be aided by driving out competing suppliers, but this is usually considered a rather inefficient and perhaps unfair way to pursue distributional objectives.

9. You do not lose your benefits upon divorce so long as you were married for at least ten years, unless you remarry. In that case, you lose your old spousal benefits (even upon re-divorce) until your new spouse dies, whereupon you can choose between past spouses to pick the highest survivor benefits.

10 In some respects, it would be easiest simply to ignore household status and apportion all taxes and benefits on an individual basis. However, this is not entirely satisfactory unless you think that, say, Mrs. Bill Gates is no better off than the average unmarried individual with the same earnings, and thus, for example, should get the same welfare benefits if she as an individual has no income.

11. The best available work on how to improve the basic structure of the current Social Security system, written before privatization and investing part of the Trust Fund in the stock market became salient political proposals, is Steuerle and Bakija (1994).

12. France and Italy have indeed made this change in response to their social security systems' financing problems (McHale 1999, 20).

13. Reischauer reports that those supporting this proposal include "such well-known Social Security experts as Henry J. Aaron, Robert M. Ball, Peter Diamond, Robert Greenstein, and Alicia H. Munnell" (1999, A-23).

14. The marginal tax rate effect would be mitigated by counting the extra covered earnings for benefit computation as well as tax purposes. However, Reischauer mentions only "rais[ing] the Social Security tax ceiling" and "subjecting a greater portion of our wages to Social Security taxes" as a way of "increas[ing] payroll tax revenues by about 4 percent" (1999, A-23).

Chapter Three

1. Even without any affect on your incentives, winning or losing overall from the Social Security system may change your decisions through what economists call income effects. For example, an expectation of receiving huge Social Security benefits upon retirement might reduce the amount that you chose to save during your working years.

2. As we will see in the next section's discussion of the issues raised by specifying a particular *r*, the forced saving program also includes a limitation on portfolio choice, since it requires participants to accept a particular investment return.

3. The income effects of Social Security's redistributive program may, however, influence an individual's preferred investment strategy as to what he or she retains.

4. The main variables, given a known real wage path and life span, concern the prospect of income taxation of benefits (depending on one's other income even if the income tax rules remain constant) and how overall wage growth will affect application of the benefit formula given wage indexing.

5. This longevity bet can be negated outside the Social Security system by purchasing life insurance (a kind of bet against your own longevity), the proceeds of which will go to your heirs.

6. The fact that Social Security only offers a life annuity rather than, say, a lump-sum payment that you could spend immediately is best seen as an aspect of forced saving.

7. The required benefit cut to restore estimated long-term fiscal balance in Social Security is smaller in percentage terms than the required tax increase because expected future benefits exceed expected future tax revenues.

Chapter Four

1. Other rationales may also support making the purchase of insurance coverage mandatory. An example is the requirement in many states that drivers have some minimum level of coverage. Here the main aim is to ensure the victims in any accident involving the driver a deep enough pocket to pay damages that are due to them.

2. Income has been defined as consumption plus change in net worth for the relevant accounting period, such as a year (Simons 1938, 50). A consumption measure leaves out the change in net worth, while a wealth measure reaches the whole of net worth at a given moment.

3. Demogrant programs tend to impose lower marginal rates on poor and near-poor households than conventional welfare programs because they do not layer on top of each other multiple income-conditioned elements, such as a benefit reduction plus income tax liability for each additional dollar earned. See Shaviro 1999. In the early 1970s, we came within hailing distance of replacing traditional welfare with a variant of the demogrant structure that had been endorsed by economists ranging from Milton Friedman on the right to James Tobin on the left and proposed by both Richard Nixon and George McGovern (Shaviro 1997b, 469–70).

4. One key difference between Harsanyi's and Rawls's treatment of the veil of ignorance is that Harsanyi argues for maximizing expected utility (which leads to a utilitarian view of social welfare) while Rawls adopts an ad hoc assumption of infinite risk aversion, suggesting that the relevant circumstances of the worst-off person in the society matter infinitely more to the observer behind the veil than those of anyone else.

5. The last two difficulties are closely related, since if you cannot offer insurance before a given risk is resolved, attempts to do so afterward will encourage adverse selection.

6. For a thorough overview of the basic distributional issues posed by family or household taxation, see Kaplow (1996).

7. Age-based adverse selection problems would arise, for example, in the fanciful case where a company that proposed to offer a fixed payout stream that would start when you reached age 70 could not observe your age until after the contract was made.

8. Even inflation-adjusted life annuities, which were not generally available in the United States until the government begin issuing indexed bonds, should now be easy to offer here if there is consumer demand for them (Brown, Mitchell, and Poterba 1999). This is the type of coverage that Social Security currently provides, and its unavailability here before the introduction of indexed bonds (which aid prospective offerors in dealing with inflation risk) was at one time advanced as a reason for Social Security (Diamond 1977, 280).

9. "Eat when you kill" might, of course, have generally been the best one could do on the savanna. Actually, our ancestors on the savanna may have been more farsighted than this, using "reciprocal altruism" (Trivers 1971), such as food sharing, to provide a kind of personal saving mechanism. Sharing your extra food today might give you a claim on others' extra food tomorrow, and thus is a form of personal saving (although not aggregate saving given the dissaving by whoever gives you a future claim by sharing your food).

10. Forced saving can, however, indirectly trigger moral hazard problems by affecting work incentives through the reduced subjective value of earning a wage.

11. However, the policy of forced saving may dictate not allowing people deliberately to make bad investment choices (so far as expected financial returns are concerned) by reason of the choices' current consumption value. An example would be betting at the racetrack because the enjoyment of doing so is worth the expected loss.

12. I say resources rather than income because here the fact that "income" generally does not take into account the value of housework performed, say, by a stay-at-home parent may be especially pertinent to comparing households' well-being. You presumably are not worse off if you rationally choose to stay home and raise your children rather than earn a wage and pay a nanny to take care of the children.

13. Why Social Security would succeed in forcing some people to save more than they want is a tougher question than it may first appear, at least within a standard economic framework based on assuming that people act on the basis of a consistent set of well-defined preferences. The two main explanations for Social Security's success in forcing some people to save more than they would on their own are (a) these individuals do not act on the basis of consistent and well-defined preferences, and thus can be steered by how the government frames their choices, and/or (b) incomplete markets make it difficult for these people to dissave on the side, for example, by effectively borrowing against the expected value of their Social Security benefits.

14. People's likely response to being "forced" into the stock market via Social Security depends in part on why they were not participating on their own. Andrew Abel suggests that deciding to participate may have an initial fixed cost (such as self-education) that some consumers decide not to bear (1998, 16). Under this view, people would have no reason to back out of the stock market once they became indirect participants via Social Security. A second explanation is that people are averse, perhaps irrationally, to stock market risk (Smetters 1999, 210). Here a conventional economic model with consistent behavior pursuant to well-defined preferences might suggest

that people would try to negate their involuntary stock market participation. This might not happen, however, if doing so is too costly or if the government can influence their behavior by how it frames their choices.

15. To be sure, if you accept the Kotlikoff-Sachs view that workers ignore the accrual of retirement benefits in any event, the cases where Social Security actually does levy a pure tax on secondary earners may not make the deterrence of work effort any worse.

Chapter Five

1. This estimate, along with all discussion of the Social Security Trust Fund in this chapter, pertains specifically to the Old-Age and Survivors Insurance (OASI) Trust Fund, the retirement (as opposed to disability) portion of Social Security that provides my exclusive focus throughout this book.

2. Under the "Ricardian" view popularized by the economist Robert Barro, transfers from future to current generations by the government might be entirely negated by offsetting resource shifts within multigenerational households. However, the consensus view is that Ricardian offsets to intergenerational transfers by the government are fairly limited (Shaviro 1997a, 68–79). A second qualification to the general claim in the text goes to the Keynesian "paradox of thrift," describing situations where the more people try to save, the less ends up being saved because national income declines due to a lack of confidence that consumer demand will recover at any foreseeable time (52–53).

3. I ignore the possible income effects of how a retirement plan is treated for income tax purposes. Tax-favoring it may conceivably reduce participants' overall saving if, for example, they are "target savers" who will save less if a tax break reduces the amount they must save to reach their targets.

4. There is strong though disputed evidence that inducing older workers to retire was a deliberate and central aim of Social Security's designers. This may have been thought to aid younger workers, although economists generally disagree that it can reduce unemployment in the long run. See Miron and Weil 1997, 17–19.

5. Henry Aaron's (1999) defense of President Clinton's proposal in terms of "modified unified budget accounting" rests on the point that, taking existing Social Security benefit commitments as given, the proposal does not actually make things worse when it counts the same dollar twice. Aaron argues that an intergovernmental transfer of bonds from the Treasury to the Trust Fund to memorialize the notional investment of the surplus would simply replace "implicit" government debt, in the form of the benefit commitments, with "explicit" debt. This is not quite descriptively accurate, since the government would hold its own newly issued debt and thus face no increased legal obligation to pay future Social Security benefits if Congress wanted to alter them in the future. Explicit debt would not really have been issued to the public. And if Congress really did issue it to replace Social Security's implicit debt, the change might worsen the government's fiscal position by making the benefits less renounceable. While Aaron is correct that the claimed double-counting as such does not make the government's fiscal situation worse, the essential reason is that the Trust Fund plays no true financing role, and thus could equally be rewritten to zero or to $100 trillion without any real effect

(apart from the possibilities of triggering a benefit cutoff or affecting perceptions about benefit affordability). His defense would equally apply to my mock proposal to count the same dollar of budget and Trust Fund surplus repeatedly until the entire implicit Social Security debt had been eliminated.

Chapter Six

1. A few commentators, such as Ferrara and Tanner, oppose forcing people to save through compulsory participation in Social Security, but even they accept that as a matter of "political reality" this feature is virtually certain to be retained (1998, 167).

2. Increased income taxation of Social Security benefits would, of course, increase overall discouragement of work by the tax-transfer system (at least if workers perceived it accurately). However, this is more or less implicit to restoring Social Security's fiscal balance through a net wage tax increase.

3. The fiscal and distributional impact of increasing the annual reach of the Social Security tax varies depending on whether the extra covered earnings are also included in AIME for benefit purposes. Even with greater benefits, high earners lose at the margin by paying more flat-rate taxes to earn more declining-rate benefits. However, if the extra covered earnings do not generate extra benefits, then the change results in a pure tax increase of 11.5 percent on the newly covered earnings—no small matter.

4. Aaron and Reischauer would, however, slightly increase spouses' survivor benefits, which now are 100 percent of the primary earner's benefit (1998, 100). This amount is two-thirds of the combined benefit for the two spouses while both are alive (100 percent plus 50 percent of the self-earned benefit), a percentage that they would increase to three-quarters. In effect, therefore, Aaron and Reischauer propose that a spouse's survivor benefit be 112.5 percent (three-quarters of 150 percent) of what a single retiree with the decedent's work history would have gotten. They do not explain why your benefits should be higher if your spouse worked and died and you now live alone, than if you worked and now live alone.

5. Earnings-sharing would also raise survivorship issues, concerning what if any earnings credited to the spouse who died first would be transferred to the surviving spouse. See Aaron and Reischauer 1998, 98.

6. A recent study suggests that, for any given year, the chance of the Trust Fund's losing money from a debt-for-stock swap is actually 20 to 25 percent, and that down years tend to occur in succession (MaCurdy and Shoven 1999).

7. Strictly speaking, the 40 percent refundable income tax differs from 40 percent stock ownership by the government because it is an income tax, rather than a consumption tax (such as a cash-flow tax on which all business outlays are immediately expensed). The income tax thus discourages saving compared to immediate consumption by the business owner in a manner that a 40 percent ownership stake would not.

8. However, due to the complicated nature of the possible general equilibrium effects of a government debt-for-stock swap, stock prices could actually either rise or fall (Diamond and Geanakoplos 1999).

9. Legislation eliminating the government's voting rights with respect to its stock would presumably also require that this stock be disregarded in applying all voting rules in corporate charters. For example, suppose that a merger proposed by management

could be blocked if one-third of all shares were voted in opposition. Management's position would be strengthened if the government's shares were implicitly counted among those not in opposition.

10. Aaron and Reischauer note that the Federal Reserve Board regulates private banks in addition to managing the money supply and has not been interfered with in this task either (1998, 111). Congress has, however, been quite active by other means in affecting banking regulation. Examples include the ongoing legislative controversies concerning the Community Reinvestment Act, which requires banks to invest in poor areas where they have branches, and the allocation of bank regulatory authority between the Federal Reserve Board and the Treasury Department (McNamee 1999).

Chapter Seven

1. Feldstein was the first to attract significant public attention to a Social Security reform plan for the United States called "privatization" (1995, 4). (The term has, however, been used to describe a similar proposal that was implemented in Chile in 1980; see Edwards 1998). Feldstein says that shifting from pay-as-you-go to full funding is his proposal's core feature, but then adds that while the funded program "could be . . . managed by the government itself, the countries that consider funded programs have proposed that the funds be invested privately, subject only to government supervision and regulation. This paper will therefore refer to the shift from an unfunded pay-as-you-go program to a funded program as privatizing social security." The name Feldstein gives to the proposed new system therefore describes what he considers a secondary feature rather than the main one.

2. While a typical defined-contribution plan is by definition fully funded (Bodie and Shoven 1983, 3), this reflects the need in private plans to have the amounts that plan participants invest actually set aside currently. One could in theory have an unfunded retirement plan in which people made notional investment choices with respect to amounts that were not actually set aside or else actually invested amounts borrowed by the plan. This could aptly be called an unfunded defined-contribution plan so long as what people got upon retirement depended on how their investment choices performed.

3. If the Archer-Shaw individual accounts had a somewhat better chance of paying off and did not require so much diversification, they would give investors an incentive to bet as riskily or even rashly as possible, since the government would have the downside.

4. The Archer-Shaw plan did, however, make the individual accounts inheritable by people who died before retirement (Stevenson 1999, A-20).

5. Since, under the Feldstein transition plan, the government merely gets back some of the money it initially put into the individual accounts, the extra financing that it receives to pay current-law benefits ($600 in the example) is best thought of as coming from general revenues, just as under President Clinton's proposal to "invest" budget surpluses in Social Security. General revenues are presumably the best candidate for the status of being the "true" marginal source of the money the government deposits in the individual accounts.

6. In general, the main ways of increasing national saving are to provide incentives

for it, shift wealth from low savers to high savers (including through transfers from present to future generations), or force people to save (such as through taxes that reduce current consumption and are used for productive long-term investment).

7. This is based on remarks Feldstein made at a workshop on Social Security at the National Bureau of Economic Research Summer Institute on August 5, 1998.

8. Even if we are optimistic about consumers' ability to look out for themselves with regard to the investment of their Social Security accounts, continued limits on portfolio choice would imply a need for regulatory oversight, since profit-seeking firms have an incentive to compete for customers by helping them to circumvent the limits.

Bibliography

Aaron, Henry J. 1966. "The Social Insurance Paradox." *Canadian Journal of Economics and Political Science* 32:371–74.

———. 1997. "A Bad Idea Whose Time Will Never Come." *Brookings Review* 15:17.

———. 1999. "The Phony Issue of Double-Counting." *Tax Notes* 82:717–19.

Aaron, Henry J., and Robert D. Reischauer. 1998. *Countdown to Reform: The Great Social Security Debate*. New York: Century Foundation Press.

Abel, Andrew B. 1998. "The Aggregate Effects of Including Equities in the Social Security Trust Fund." National Bureau of Economic Research Summer Institute: Risk and Distribution Issues in Social Security Reform, August 5.

Achenbaum, W. Andrew. 1986. *Social Security: Visions and Revisions*. Cambridge: Cambridge University Press.

Advisory Council on Social Security. 1997. *Findings and Recommendations*. Vol. 1, *Final Report of the 1994–1996 Advisory Council on Social Security*. Washington, D.C.: Social Security Administration.

Angelis, Theodore J. 1998. "Investing Public Money in Private Markets: What Are the Right Questions?" In *Framing the Social Security Debate: Values, Politics, and Economics*, edited by R. Douglas Arnold, Michael J. Graetz, and Alicia H. Munnell. Washington, D.C.: National Academy of Social Insurance.

Atkinson, Anthony B. 1987. "Income Maintenance and Social Insurance." In *Handbook of Public Economics*, edited by Alan J. Auerbach and Martin Feldstein. Vol. 2. Amsterdam: North-Holland.

———. 1995. *Incomes and the Welfare State*. Cambridge: Cambridge University Press.

Auerbach, Alan J., and Laurence J. Kotlikoff. 1995. *Macroeconomics: An Integrated Approach*. Cincinnati: South-Western College Publishing.

Baker, Dean, and Mark Weisbrot. 1999. *Social Security: The Phony Crisis*. Chicago: University of Chicago Press.

Ball, Robert M, with Thomas N. Bethell. 1998. *Straight Talk About Social Security: An Analysis of the Issues in the Current Debate*. New York: Century Foundation Press.

Bankman, Joseph, and Thomas Griffith. 1987. "Social Welfare and the Rate Structure: A New Look at Progressive Taxation." *California Law Review* 75:1905–67.

Barr, Nicholas. 1993. *The Economics of the Welfare State*. Stanford: Stanford University Press.

Berle, Adolph, Jr., and Gardiner C. Means. 1932. *The Modern Corporation and Private Property*. New York: Macmillan.

Bierce, Ambrose. 1993 edition. *The Devil's Dictionary*. New York: Dover Publications.

Black, Bernard S. 1998. "Shareholder Activism and Corporate Governance in the United States." In *The New Palgrave Dictionary of Economics and the Law*, edited by Peter Newman. Vol. 3. London: Macmillan Reference Limited.

Bodie, Zvi. 1999. "Financial Engineering and Social Security Reform." Paper delivered at an NBER conference, Islamorada, Fla., January 16.

Bodie, Zvi, and John B. Shoven, eds.. 1983. "Introduction." In *Financial Aspects of the United States Pension System*. Chicago: University of Chicago Press.

Boskin, Michael J., Ellen R. Dulberger, Robert J. Gordon, Zvi Griliches, and Dale W. Jorgenson. 1996. "Toward a More Accurate Measure of the Cost of Living." Final Report to the Senate Finance Committee, December 4.

Bosworth, Barry P. 1996. "Fund Accumulation: How Much? How Managed?" In *Social Security: What Role for the Future?*, edited by Peter A. Diamond, David C. Lindeman, and Howard Young. Washington, D.C.: National Academy of Social Insurance.

Brown, Jeffrey R., Olivia S. Mitchell, and James M. Poterba. 1999. "The Role of Real Annuities and Indexed Bonds in an Individual Accounts Retirement Program." NBER Working Paper no. 7005.

Caldwell, Steven, Melissa Favreault, Alla Gantman, Jagadeesh Gokhale, Thomas Johnson, and Laurence J. Kotlikoff. 1999. "Social Security's Treatment of Postwar Americans." In *Tax Policy and the Economy*, edited by James M. Poterba. Vol. 13. Cambridge, Mass.: National Bureau of Economic Research.

Committee on Ways and Means, U.S. House of Representatives. 1996. *1996 Green Book: Background Material and Data on Programs within the Jurisdiction of the Committee on Ways and Means*. Washington, D.C.: U.S. Government Printing Office.

Coronado, Julia Lynn, Don Fullerton, and Thomas Glass. 1999. "Distributional Impacts of Proposed Changes to the Social Security System." In *Tax Policy and the Economy*, edited by James M. Poterba. Vol. 13. Cambridge, Mass.: National Bureau of Economic Research.

Delgado, Richard, and Jean Stefancic. 1992. "Symposium: Images of the Outsider in American Law and Culture: Can Free Expression Remedy Systemic Social Ills?" *Cornell Law Review* 77:1258.

Derthick, Martha. 1979. *Policymaking for Social Security*. Washington, D.C.: Brookings Institution.

Diamond, Peter A. 1977. "A Framework for Social Security Analysis." *Journal of Public Economics* 8:275–98.

———. 1999. "Administrative Costs and Equilibrium Charges with Individual Accounts." NBER Working Paper no. 7050. Diamond, Peter A., and John Geanakoplos. 1999. "Social Security Investment in Equities I: Linear Case." NBER Working Paper no. 7103.

Donmoyer, Ryan J. 1999. "Lawmakers Continue Social Security Posturing." *Tax Notes* 83:607–8.

Edwards, Sebastian. 1998. "The Chilean Pension Reform: A Pioneering Program." In

Privatizing Social Security, edited by Martin Feldstein. Chicago: University of Chicago Press.

Eisner, Robert. 1998. *Social Security: More Not Less*. New York: Century Foundation Press.

Engen, Eric M., and William G. Gale. 1997. "The Effects of Social Security Reform on Private and National Saving." In *Social Security Reform: Links to Saving, Investment, and Growth*, edited by Steven A. Sass and Robert K. Triest. Boston: Federal Reserve Bank of Boston.

Feldstein, Martin. 1974. "Social Security, Induced Retirement, and Aggregate Capital Accumulation." *Journal of Political Economy* 82:75–95.

———. 1995. "Would Privatizing Social Security Raise Economic Welfare?" NBER Working Paper no. 5281.

———. 1996. "Social Security and Saving: New Time Series Evidence." *National Tax Journal* 49:151–64.

———, ed. 1998. "Introduction." In *Privatizing Social Security*. Chicago: University of Chicago Press.

———. 1999a. "Clinton's Social Security Sham." *Wall Street Journal*, February 1, p. A-20.

———. 1999b. "Social Security Reform: America's Golden Opportunity." *The Economist*, March 13, pp. 41–43.

Feldstein, Martin, and Elena Ranguelova. 1999. "The Economics of Bequests in Pensions and Social Security." NBER Working Paper no. 7065.

Feldstein, Martin, Elena Ranguelova, and Andrew Samwick. 1999. "The Transition to Investment-Based Social Security When Portfolio Returns and Capital Profitability Are Uncertain." NBER Working Paper no. 7016.

Feldstein, Martin, and Andrew Samwick. 1998. "The Transition Path in Privatizing Social Security." In *Privatizing Social Security*, edited by Martin Feldstein. Chicago: University of Chicago Press.

———. 1999. "Maintaining Social Security Benefits and Tax Rates through Personal Retirement Accounts: An Update Based on the 1998 Social Security Trustees' Report." National Bureau of Economic Research.

Ferrara, Peter J., and Michael Tanner. 1998. *A New Deal for Social Security*. Washington, D.C.: Cato Institute.

Friedberg, Leora. 1999. "The Labor Supply Effects of the Social Security Earnings Test." NBER Working Paper no. 7200.

Friedman, Milton. 1957. *A Theory of the Consumption Function*. Princeton: Princeton University Press.

———. 1999. "Social Security Socialism." *Wall Street Journal*, January 26, p. A-18.

Friedman, Thomas L. 1997. "Oops! Wrong War." *New York Times*, April 7, p. A-15.

Geanakoplos, John, Olivia S. Mitchell, and Stephen P. Zeldes. 1998. "Would a Privatized Social Security System Really Pay a Higher Rate of Return?" NBER Working Paper no. 6713.

———. 1999. "Social Security Money's Worth." In *Prospects for Social Security Reform*, edited by Olivia S. Mitchell, Robert J. Myers, and Howard Young. Philadelphia: University of Pennsylvania Press.

Glassman, James K., and Kevin Hassett. 1999. *Dow 36,000: The New Strategy for Profiting from the Coming Rise in the Stock Market.* New York: Times Books.

Goldberg, Fred T., Jr., and Michael J. Graetz. 1999. "Reforming Social Security: A Practical and Workable System of Personal Retirement Accounts." NBER Working Paper no. 6970.

Goss, Stephen C. 1999. "Measuring Solvency in the Social Security System." In *Prospects for Social Security Reform*, edited by Olivia S. Mitchell, Robert J. Myers, and Howard Young. Philadelphia: University of Pennsylvania Press.

Gramlich, Edward M. 1998. *Is It Time to Reform Social Security?* Ann Arbor: University of Michigan Press.

Gravelle, Jane G. 1998. "The Marriage Penalty and Other Family Tax Issues." Congressional Research Service Paper no. 98-653E. Washington, D.C.: Library of Congress.

Harsanyi, John C. 1953. "Cardinal Utility in Welfare Economics and in the Theory of Risk-Taking." *Journal of Political Economy* 61:434–35.

Ip, Greg. 1999. "Can Social Security Funds Be Invested Free of Politics?" *Wall Street Journal*, January 22, p. C-1.

Ippolito, Richard A. 1999. Review of *Privatizing Social Security*, edited by Martin Feldstein. *National Tax Journal* 52:139–44.

Jacobs, W. W. 1998 ed. *The Monkey's Paw and Other Tales of Mystery and the Macabre.* Chicago: Academy Chicago Publishers.

James, Estelle, Gary Ferrier, James Smallhout, and Dimitri Vittas. 1999. "Mutual Funds and Institutional Investments: What Is the Most Efficient Way to Set Up Individual Accounts in a Social Security System?" NBER Working Paper no. 7049.

Kahneman, Daniel, and Amos Tversky. 1979. "Prospect Theory: An Analysis of Decision Under Risk." *Econometrica* 47:263–92.

Kaplow, Louis. 1991. "The Income Tax as Insurance: The Casualty Loss and Medical Expense Deductions and the Exclusion of Medical Insurance Premiums." *California Law Review* 79:1485–510.

———. 1996. "Optimal Distribution and the Family." *Scandinavian Journal of Economics* 98 (1): 75–92.

Keynes, John Maynard. 1964 ed. *The General Theory of Employment, Interest, and Money.* San Diego: Harcourt Brace & Company.

Kotlikoff, Laurence J. 1992 *Generational Accounting: Knowing Who Pays, and When, for What We Spend.* New York: The Free Press.

Kotlikoff, Laurence J., and Jeffrey Sachs. 1997. "It's High Time to Privatize." *Brookings Review* 15:16.

Lawrance, Emily. 1991. "Poverty and the Rate of Time Preference: Evidence from Panel Data." *Journal of Political Economy* 99:54.

MaCurdy, Thomas E., and John B. Shoven. 1999. "Asset Allocation and Risk Allocation: Can Social Security Improve Its Future Solvency Problems by Investing in Private Securities?" NBER Working Paper no. 7015.

McCaffery, Edward J. 1997. *Taxing Women.* Chicago: University of Chicago Press.

McHale, John. 1999. "The Risk of Social Security Benefit Rule Changes: Some International Evidence." NBER Working Paper no. 7031.

McNamee, Mike. 1999. "Banking Reform or Bust: Senator Gramm Ups the Ante." *Business Week*, May 24, p. 43.

Mehra, Rajnish, and Edward C. Prescott. 1985. "The Equity Premium: A Puzzle." *Journal of Monetary Economics* 15:145–162.

Merton, Robert C. 1983. "On the Role of Social Security as a Means for Efficient Risk Sharing in an Economy Where Human Capital Is Not Tradeable." In *Financial Aspects of the United States Pension System*, edited by Zvi Bodie and John B. Shoven. Chicago: University of Chicago Press.

Miron, Jeffrey A., and David N. Weil. 1997. "The Genesis and Evolution of Social Security." NBER Working Paper no. 5949.

Mirrlees, James. 1971. "An Exploration in the Theory of Optimum Income Taxation." *Review of Economic Studies* 38:175–208.

Mitchell, Daniel. 1999. "GOP Offers a Social Security Plan Worse Than Clinton's." *Wall Street Journal*, May 3, p. A-22.

Mitchell, Olivia S. 1998. "Administrative Costs in Public and Private Retirement Systems." In *Privatizing Social Security*, edited by Martin Feldstein. Chicago: University of Chicago Press.

Modigliani, Franco, and Richard Brumberg. 1954. "Utility Analysis and the Consumption Function: An Interpretation of Cross-Section Data." In *Post Keynesian Economics*, edited by K. K. Kurihara. New Brunswick, N.J.: Rutgers University Press.

Mulligan, Casey R., and Xavier Sala-i-Martin. 1999a. "Gerontocracy, Retirement, and Social Security." NBER Working Paper no. 7117.

———. 1999b. "Social Security in Theory and Practice (I): Facts and Political Theories." NBER Working Paper no. 7118.

———. 1999c. "Social Security in Theory and Practice (II): Efficiency Theories, Narrative Theories, and Implications for Reform." NBER Working Paper no. 7119.

Munnell, Alicia H., and Pierluigi Balduzzi. 1998. "Investing the Social Security Trust Funds in Equities." Washington, D.C.: Public Policy Institute, American Association of Retired Persons.

Murray, Alan. 1999. "Clinton Plays to Aging Boomers." *Wall Street Journal*, March 29, p. A-1.

Poterba, James M., and David A. Wise. 1998. "Individual Financial Decisions in Retirement Savings Plans and the Provision of Resources for Retirement." In *Privatizing Social Security*, edited by Martin Feldstein. Chicago: University of Chicago Press.

Rawls, John. 1971. *A Theory of Justice*. Cambridge: Harvard University Press.

Reischauer, Robert D. 1999. "The 75-Year Plan." *New York Times*, April 9, p. A-23.

Romano, Roberta. 1993. "Public Pension Fund Activism in Corporate Governance Reconsidered." *Columbia Law Review* 93:795–852.

Rosen, Harvey S. 1995. *Public Finance*. 4th ed. Chicago: Richard D. Irwin.

Samuelson, Paul A. 1958. "An Exact Consumption-Loan Model of Interest with or without the Social Contrivance of Money." *Journal of Political Economy* 66:467–82.

———. 1983. "Comment." In *Financial Aspects of the United States Pension System*, edited by Zvi Bodie and John B. Shoven. Chicago: University of Chicago Press.

Seidman, Laurence S. 1999. *Funding Social Security: A Strategic Alternative*. Cambridge: Cambridge University Press.

Shaviro, Daniel. 1997a. *Do Deficits Matter?* Chicago: University of Chicago Press.

———. 1997b. "The Minimum Wage, the Earned Income Tax Credit, and Optimal Subsidy Policy." *University of Chicago Law Review* 64:405–81.

———. 1999. "Effective Marginal Tax Rates on Low-Income Households." *Tax Notes* 84:1191–1201.

———. 2000. *When Rules Change: An Economic and Political Analysis of Transition Relief and Retroactivity.* Chicago: University of Chicago Press.

Shiller, Robert J. 1993. *Macro Markets: Creating Institutions for Managing Society's Largest Economic Risks.* New York: Oxford University Press.

———. 1998. "Social Security and Institutions for Intergenerational, Intragenerational and International Risk Sharing." NBER Summer Institute: Risk and Distribution Issues in Social Security Reform, August 5.

Shogan, Robert. 1995. "Dole Joins Supply-Siders as Last Great GOP Convert." *Los Angeles Times*, September 6, p. A-1.

Siegel, Jeremy J. 1992. "The Equity Premium: Stock and Bond Returns Since 1802." *Financial Analysts Journal* 48:28–38.

Siegel, Jeremy J., and Richard H. Thaler. 1997. "Anomalies: The Equity Premium Puzzle." *Journal of Economic Perspectives* 11 (1): 191–200.

Simons, Henry C. 1938. *Personal Income Taxation.* Chicago: University of Chicago Press.

Smetters, Kent A. 1999. "Thinking About Social Security's Trust Fund." In *Prospects for Social Security Reform,* edited by Olivia S. Mitchell, Robert J. Myers, and Howard Young. Philadelphia: University of Pennsylvania Press.

Steuerle, C. Eugene, and Jon M. Bakija. 1994. *Retooling Social Security for the 21st Century: Right and Wrong Approaches to Reform.* Washington, D.C.: Urban Institute Press.

Steuerle, C. Eugene, Edward M. Gramlich, Hugh Heclo, and Demetra Smith Nightingale. 1998. *The Government We Deserve: Responsive Democracy and Changing Expectations.* Washington, D.C.: Urban Institute Press.

Stevenson, Richard W. 1999. "Two Key Republicans Press Ahead on Social Security, Offering Investment-Account Plan." *New York Times*, April 29, p. A-20.

Trivers, Robert. 1971. "The Evolution of Reciprocal Altruism." *Quarterly Review of Biology* 46:35–56.

United States General Accounting Office. 1998. *Social Security Financing: Implications of Government Stock Investing for the Trust Fund, the Federal Budget, and the Economy.* Washington, D.C.: Government Printing Office.

Varian, Hal R. 1980. "Redistributive Taxation as Social Insurance." *Journal of Public Economics* 14:49–68.

Wilde, Oscar. 1948 ed. "The Model Millionaire." In *Complete Works of Oscar Wilde.* London: Collins Clear-Type Press.

Wilson, James Q. 1991. *Bureaucracy: What Government Agencies Do and Why They Do It.* New York: Basic Books.

Wodehouse, P. G. 1975 ed. *The Code of the Woosters.* New York: Vintage Books.

Index

McNamee, Mike, 165
Means, Gardiner, 119–21
means-testing, 49
Medicaid, 142
Medicare, 11, 48, 54, 58, 61, 124
Mehra, Rajnish, 98
Merton, Robert, 64, 82
Miron, Jeffrey, 90, 160, 163
Mirrlees, James, 52
Mitchell, Daniel, 135
Mitchell, Olivia, 68, 98, 127, 162
Modigliani, Franco, 60
money machines, 129–32
moral hazard, 46, 55, 57, 58, 63, 65, 73, 119
Mother Teresa, 10
Mulligan, Casey, 67, 91, 139
Munnell, Alicia, 122, 160
Murray, Alan, 91

national saving, 79–82, 84–87, 128, 131–32, 135–37, 144, 149, 151
New Deal, 2
Nixon, Richard, 20, 161

paternalism, 47, 60, 103
pay-as-you-go funding, 82, 84–85
Penner, Rudolph, 91
PIA. *See* primary insurance amount
portfolio choice. *See* limited portfolio choice in Social Security
Poterba, James, 138, 162
Prescott, Edward, 98
primary insurance amount, 14–15
private insurance, 42, 44–47, 54–56, 73–74
private versus public retirement plans, 23, 77–79, 89–90, 99, 149
privatization of Social Security: and administrative costs, 126–27, 139–42, 145, 151; compared to investing the Trust Fund in the stock market, 138–39; compared to privatizing standard economic production, 126–27, 144; definition of, 126–29; and full funding of benefits, 131–32, 135–36; and household issues, 143–44; and individual accounts, 132–35, 145, 166; and national saving, 4, 130–32, 135–37, 144, 151; as a package of distinct policy changes, 4–5, 101, 128–29, 151; and political risk, 133; and portfolio choice, 4, 137–40, 145, 151, 166; and redistribution, 5, 142–43, 145, 151–52; role of private investment firms under, 139–42, 166; transition to, 129–

32; use of a "money machine" to pay for, 129–32
progressive privatization, 152–56
progressive redistribution: under current Social Security system, 15, 69–71, 74, 104–5; under privatization, 5, 142–43; under progressive privatization, 153–55

Ranguelova, Elena, 131, 143–44, 156
Rawls, John, 52, 161
redistribution through Social Security: between high-earners and low-earners, 5, 15, 23, 69–71; between households, 72–73; between men and women, 15; between short-lived and long-lived individuals, 15; in general: 3, 22, 31, 62–65, 69–74; intergenerational, 5, 25–27, 33, 40–42, 63–64, 71–72, 149; under privatization, 4, 142–43; under progressive privatization, 153–55
Reischauer, Robert, 22, 31, 101, 108, 110, 113, 118, 121–22, 132, 140, 160, 164–65
retirement ages in Social Security, 15–16, 106–7
retirement and part-time work, 16–17
Ricardianism, 163
risk premia, 35
risk prevention, 4, 47–48, 60–61, 74, 149
risk-return frontier, 35–38, 62
risk-spreading, 4, 45, 47–48, 74, 149
Romano, Roberta, 122
Roosevelt, President Franklin, 40, 90–91, 99
Rosen, Harvey, 48, 49
"Rube Goldberg" characteristics of Social Security, 10, 19, 124, 150

Sachs, Jeffrey, 12–13, 21, 31–32, 105, 109, 127, 163
Sala-i-Martin, Xavier, 67, 91, 139
Samuelson, Paul, 81, 84, 85
Samwick, Andrew, 92, 129, 131
saving. *See* forced saving by individuals through Social Security; national saving
"saving" Social Security, 1, 5, 24, 32, 75, 147, 157
Seidman, Laurence, 81
Shaviro, Daniel, 56, 71, 81, 91, 122, 142, 157
Shaw, Clay (congressman), 134–35, 165
Shiller, Robert, 45, 49, 51, 55, 60, 64
Shogan, Robert, 22
Shoven, John, 83, 164, 165
Siegel, Jeremy, 98, 135